The Complete Guide To Writing Effective College Applications And Essays

Step by Step Instructions with Companion CD

REVISED 2ND EDITION

By Kathy Hahn

Revised by Debra Lipphardt

THE COMPLETE GUIDE TO WRITING EFFECTIVE COLLEGE APPLICATIONS AND ESSAYS: STEP BY STEP INSTRUCTIONS WITH COMPANION CD - REVISED 2ND EDITION

Copyright © 2016 Atlantic Publishing Group, Inc.
1405 SW 6th Avenue • Ocala, Florida 34471 • Phone 800-814-1132 • Fax 352-622-1875
Web site: www.atlantic-pub.com • E-mail: sales@atlantic-pub.com
SAN Number: 268-1250

Library of Congress Cataloging-in-Publication Data

Names: Hahn, Kathy L. (Kathy Lynn), 1957- | Lipphardt, Debra, 1954-
Title: The complete guide to writing effective college applications and
   essays : step-by-step instructions with companion CD-ROM / by Kathy L.
   Hahn; revised by Debra Lipphardt.
Description: Revised second edition. | Ocala, Florida : Atlantic Publishing
   Group, Inc., [2015] | Includes bibliographical references and index.
Identifiers: LCCN 2015036449| ISBN 9781620231173 (alk. paper) | ISBN
   1620231174 (alk. paper)
Subjects: LCSH: College applications--Handbooks, manuals, etc. |
   Essay--Authorship--Problems, exercises, etc. | Rhetoric. | Universities
   and colleges--Admission.
Classification: LCC LB2351.5 .H34 2015 | DDC 378.1/616--dc23 LC record available at https://lccn.
loc.gov/2015036449

Printed in the United States

EDITOR: Rebekah Sack • rsack@atlantic-pub.com
INTERIOR LAYOUT: Antoinette D'Amore • addesign@videotron.ca
COVER DESIGN: Meg Buchner • meg@megbuchner.com
JACKET DESIGN: Justin Oefelein • justin.o@spxmultimedia.com

Printed on Recycled Paper

Reduce. Reuse.
RECYCLE.

A decade ago, Atlantic Publishing signed the Green Press Initiative. These guidelines promote environmentally friendly practices, such as using recycled stock and vegetable-based inks, avoiding waste, choosing energy-efficient resources, and promoting a no-pulping policy. We now use 100-percent recycled stock on all our books. The results: in one year, switching to post-consumer recycled stock saved 24 mature trees, 5,000 gallons of water, the equivalent of the total energy used for one home in a year, and the equivalent of the greenhouse gases from one car driven for a year.

Over the years, we have adopted a number of dogs from rescues and shelters. First there was Bear and after he passed, Ginger and Scout. Now, we have Kira, another rescue. They have brought immense joy and love not just into our lives, but into the lives of all who met them.

We want you to know a portion of the profits of this book will be donated in Bear, Ginger and Scout's memory to local animal shelters, parks, conservation organizations, and other individuals and nonprofit organizations in need of assistance.

– Douglas & Sherri Brown,
President & Vice-President of Atlantic Publishing

❦

Table of Contents

Introduction

For many students, the thought of going to college is a harrowing, nail-biting quandary. Students may ask themselves: *What am I doing? How can I accomplish this? How am I going to get in? Where will I go? What will I do once I get there? What is my major?* These questions are only a few of many that will soon be addressed, and it is often difficult to find easy answers. Nothing worthwhile in life ever comes easily, and there will always be a reason to nibble at those nails; the college decision will be one of the more important, because it reaps a harvest that will last a lifetime.

With any luck, you and your parents have been communicating about this decision, and they have been supportive and yet respectful of your need to think for yourself, but the college dilemma can be made even worse by continual questions from well-meaning relatives, teachers, and friends — especially those who frame their questions with a definite bias: such as Uncle Joe, who encourages you to attend his college.

Uncle Joe: "So, have you decided where you would like to go to school? You know, Ohio State has the best football team. It's my old alma mater, and they also have some of the best tailgating parties."

Or

Mrs. Dunne (one of your teachers): "Isn't your sister at Iowa State? Wouldn't you like to go where you she is? After all, she is quite intelligent, and if she chose Iowa, perhaps you too should think about it?"

Or

Your best friend: "You should go to Hollins with me. That way we can room together and still have great times!"

Or

Mom and/or Dad: "We really do not think that you are ready to leave home yet. I mean, who will make your meals, do your laundry, or clean your room? You are not grown up enough. You might stay out too late or go to too many parties."

Before I continue, I should emphasize that, despite some humorous sidebars and a truly laid-back approach, this book is directed toward students who intend to make the most of the educational opportunity, because that is the most important reason for going to college. This does not mean you cannot enjoy Uncle Joe's football games or tailgate parties; however, they should not be the final determining factor in whether Ohio State would be right — or wrong — for you. Buckeye games and tailgate parties are optional; you can choose to go or steer clear. The thing to consider first and foremost is: does Ohio State offer the program you want?

Let me say this, right up front: if in all honesty the tailgate-party opportunity is indeed your No. 1 priority, you might as well forget about college; you can find a minimum-wage hard-labor job and party all you want for much less money and effort. It is also a good way to go set yourself up for failure, waste a lot of money, and then return home with your tail between your legs. Furthermore, you are clearing up a space for a student who in reality does want to attend and make the most of the opportunity. Yet, if you are looking forward to those parties as an occasional means of recreation and socializing amid studies for a professional and rewarding career, this indicates a healthy balance and is no indication that you will not succeed. Uncle Joe would probably agree; he just likes to tease you with boasting of his parties because he is trying to be "cool" and show he identifies with you. It's annoying, but his intentions are good.

And what of your other college-aspiration inquisitors? Although Mrs. Dunne has been a positive influence throughout your high school days and has always complimented your work to the highest degree, she never could quite understand that references to Judy — and there have been many — always made you uncomfortable. The thought of attending yet another school in which you might always be asked "How is Judy?" and compared to her simply does not interest you — especially because you do not actually want an MFA; you are more into journalism than the fine arts. (Let's not even mention that you find the mountains of Missoula, Montana and the University of Montana's well-renowned School of Journalism far more appealing than endless cornfields surrounding Iowa City.)

As far as your best friend or boyfriend is concerned, this may be a little tougher, emotionally speaking, but the truth is you will miss him if he goes away to school but — trust me — you cannot base the rest of your life and on your best friends' desires. It has to be what is best for you, not them.

And in this day of text messaging, emailing and free long-distance cell phones, even if college takes you in different directions, you are in reality never going to lose touch with those you care about. Again, this should not be a deciding factor unless the educational benefits warrant it.

Along these lines, you must also keep in mind that the college experience will glean many more friendships and acquaintances — new people to join the network of everyone who has thus far befriended and influenced you up to this point in your life. Your present circle, formed by the first 17-19 years, will soon be aligned with a new circle, which will in turn expand and lead to more ... these circles will eventually begin to intersect (think of the Olympic logo or the inevitable Venn diagrams in math class), and you will one day find that you have developed and are part of a wonderful system of human support. Meeting new people does not mean abandoning the old; rather, the combination of both will provide a wider base of emotional support and offer many different avenues of resource further down the road, when college is just a memory and you are helping your own child go through this stage — but, hey, let's get *your* degree first.

Although I have already stated (and restated) that educational goals should be the first concern, there are many factors to weigh that go into the process of choosing and applying to colleges — including social and networking opportunities. These factors include cost, location, academic expectations, extracurricular opportunities, the "feel" of the college (which can only be demonstrated by actually visiting the campus), plus — of course — acceptance of you as a student. And because an overview is always advisable, we shall briefly explore those preliminary questions in the next five chapters. However, discussing those issues is not the primary intention of this book; the relative brevity of Chapters 1 through 5 will attest to that.

Beginning with Chapter 6, we are going to delve into what for many is the most "frightening" aspect of college application: the application essay.

Please notice the quotation marks around that adjective. The application essay is nothing to fear — at least, no more than any other challenge you will face along the way. And let me state for the record, unequivocally and irrevocably, right here and now: **college will require writing**. A veritable boatload of it. The application essay is just the beginning... and if the notion of a plethora of writing *truly* frightens you, you may need or want to rethink your decision to go to college.

But wait — let's not confuse "fright" with "laziness." If you feel exhausted just thinking about the essays, as opposed to trembling or breaking out in hives, you will most likely end up doing fine. Writing is like anything else. With a little practice and stretching of the figurative creative muscles, you will soon find it easier. Chapters 7 through 9 more thoroughly discuss what the admissions committees look for, and Chapter 10 is devoted to brain-storming ideas. Chapters 11 through 13 share some of my tips and suggestions for doing that most basic-yet-seemingly daunting of tasks: writing, and especially how it applies to the essay. I will do my best to convince you why penmanship is so critical, and I will also introduce you to a few more ideas that may not have not occurred to you.

Chapter 14, written by my co-author, Colleen M. Loew, summarizes and reiterates many of the key points covered in the first 13 chapters and also adds fresh advice and new perspectives. No two writers will embrace the exact same techniques or writing styles, and this is a good way for you to begin to see that. Perhaps find her ideas and tips more to your liking.

Appendix I is a collection of mini-essays that actually developed into the equivalent of a grad-school application essay for me. I have included it for several reasons: 1) It reveals many of the concepts of self-reflection that I discuss in Chapter 1, and 2) It represents a case of how a superficial reading might result in an admission committee's overlooking the fact that what I expressed actually fit quite well into the school's Jesuit philosophies. It is the responsibility of the admissions committee to read and interpret these essays; therefore, it will not go unnoticed if you submit something of depth and meaning.

One note of caution: the opinions I express in my essay(s) are totally my own. Neither my publisher nor co-author should be held accountable if your personal beliefs are offended. And I have no intention to offend; I am merely stating my beliefs (as we all have the right to do) and answering the questions as they were asked.

Appendix II provides a starter list of scholarship websites. Please bear in mind that even if the site talks about, for example, "Spring 2014," this is likely a repeating scholarship offer, and it will do well for you to look more closely. One of the best ways to do this is to search for the title of the scholarship along with the current year.

This book also contains a bibliography that includes a host of related works on the subject of college admissions and application essays. Most of these books are inexpensive and can either be checked out from your local library or purchased online for minimal cost. There is no "right" and all-encompassing work; each one (like this, I hope) can contribute valuable advice to your overall college application strategy.

A final few words of introduction: In this book, I have attempted not so much to give you the official, formal how-to's of the full college application process. As the bibliography will attest, there are many books and articles on that subject written by people far more informed and than I am. What I am hoping to do here, and in a kind and gentle way, is offer a more practical and conversational look at the realities of some of the challenges you will face (especially when it comes to writing) and how best to address them. I want to talk frankly and casually, and I will also try to stay away from technicalities as much as possible — you will hear enough of them from other sources.

This is not a book that you need to memorize, or one that you will be quizzed on later; rather, it is an informal tool to help start you on the way. After reading this, you may want to investigate further into the more detailed "nuts and bolts" of the process, and the works listed in the bibliography are just a handful of the tools that are out there to help you. Drawing upon the expertise of real-life case histories, my co-author's contributions, and my own experience as a college student, college composition instructor, editor, and writer, this book will help guide you — at least long enough to let your fingernails grow back — along the first steps of your college-bound journey.

Chapter 1

Is College the Right Choice for You?

o you recall your eighth grade year? By the time you begin reading this book, I am sure that you are well past that period, but this watershed year of your school life is where it all began: the college admissions preparation process. You most likely did not even realize it at the time, but it all started that day that you selected your first ninth-grade high school classes. If you were anything like me, you had already developed an affinity for a particular subject or area of interest, such as science, math, art, or English. I was strong in social studies and even more so in English, and therefore, the high school guidance counselor determined that I would be best suited for accelerated English coursework in my freshman year.

At any rate, the first few days of my freshman classes were quite over-whelming, especially because I was in a new school with many classmates from other feeder junior-high or middle schools. Always somewhat of an introvert, I was content to blend into the chalkboard and listen while other students freely volunteered their opinions and thoughts of the summer reading we had been required. Whenever someone offered a comment or made an observation, I found myself secretly wondering: *Why didn't I think of that?*

Despite my already-proven English skills, I never felt that anything I had to say would be as intelligent or meaningful as the others — and if by any chance I did think of something, it seemed that someone would always beat me to the punch, mainly because I was too shy to raise my hand. This reticence and uncertainty proved to be a problem, because my enthusiastic and brilliant teacher insisted upon making us work extremely hard for our grades, and "work" included regular input to classroom discussion.

Class participation was critical, and I felt I was nowhere near ready to provide any type of worthwhile contribution. It was not that I did not read the material or was unprepared for class; rather, I did not want to make a fool of myself in front of the teacher and my classmates. Typical of most grade- and middle-school students, I had received my fair share of teasing (for reasons both real and imagined), and the resulting embarrassment had led me into the "keep-a-low-profile" approach to school. If I did not say or do anything, I would not be made fun of, right?

Unfortunately, I found that Mrs. G was dead serious about the participation, and my early grades suffered because of it. I was dismayed that all my papers would come back nothing short of "excellent" or "good job" in the margins and the all-critical "A" at the top, but my overall grade was still in the lower "B" range. I knew I was not content with that sort of English grade (had it been math, my mother would have thrown me a confetti parade and declared a national holiday), but I just could not overcome the shyness barrier.

Then, one day shortly after the Christmas break, Mrs. G was reading aloud and analyzing line-by-line Edward Arlington Robinson's poem "Richard Cory." When she came to the part that said: "But still he fluttered pulses when he said, / 'Good morning,' and he glittered when he walked." After this stanza-ending line, she paused and said, "'Fluttered pulses' ... I never really understood that line."

Without even thinking, my hand shot up and I exclaimed, "Oh, that means that women still swooned or felt faint when he spoke to them" — even more, I gave a melodramatic Aunt Pittypat-gesture of fanning myself ... "Ooohhh, Richard Cory spoke to me."

Mrs. G could not believe this extemporaneous and unexpected response, but she was wise enough not to overplay her reaction, which in all likelihood would have driven me back into the chalkboard for good: "Oh, my goodness, Kathy — I never thought of that. Of course that is what it means; funny, it just never occurred to me. Okay, now let's take the next line ..." Even some of the other students were nodding, and amazingly enough, nobody made fun of me. (And yes, from then on, I felt comfortable participating in discussions — perhaps even too much at times.)

All kidding aside, the important thing was that — in that one crystal moment — I suddenly realized that I was every bit as capable as anyone else of making worthwhile feedback to the classes I truly loved. I knew Mrs. G wanted us all to participate, but even after I broke out of my chalk dust shell, I still did not see why it mattered so much. What I could not possibly understand at the time was that she was doing the one thing that many other teachers failed to recognize or did not want to deal with, and that was to prepare her students for what was to be the college experience. By encouraging — no, demanding — participation and an overall interest in the course, she was doing what she thought was best to "weed out" those of us who could excel in college opposed to those who would merely coast by, or those who would fail or never attend college. When I entered some of my first college classes, it was, as Yogi Berra would say, "like déjà vu of high school freshman English all over again" — but this time, thanks to Mrs. G and the other fine AP high school English teachers I had, I was well-prepared.

This story leads to the following question that may appear incredibly simple on the surface, but it's one that leads to many others more difficult to answer: Is college the right choice for you? The key to resolving this issue must first be explored with a bit of self-reflection, beginning with asking the following questions of yourself:

- Who am I? Where do I come from? Where do I want to go in life? How successful do I want to be?

- What are my talents? What are my strengths?
  What are my weaknesses?
- Do I like school? Do I put forth my best effort in school?
- What kinds of extracurricular activities do I enjoy?
- Will my skills be best put to use in college?
- What do I want to be when I grow up, and will college
  help me get there?

These important initial questions must be asked (and there are many others to come) when addressing the issue of college and when contemplating how to proceed with the college application process.

These questions require a period of personal reflection, which could take a goodly amount of time. Though, the most important thing to bear in mind is that you must use this as a means by which to make the decision on your own whether or not to attend college. This should not be dictated by somebody else, and it should not be dependent on where your friends decide to go to college, or what school(s) your parents, relatives, or siblings attended. This choice should be purely personal, and it should reveal who you are as a person and the type of growth that you would like to achieve. You must also be honest with yourself (hey, you will know up front if you are lying, and everybody else will soon find out) and willing to admit that there are areas in which you would be fooling yourself — and therefore cheating yourself — if you were to be anything other than truthful.

The identification of personal strengths and weaknesses will be difficult for some of you. After being told all your life that bragging is not appropriate, or that modesty is an admirable trait, you may hesitate to "toot your own horn" by calling attention to your most dominant assets (such as *I am in the top 5 percent of my class or I am the varsity quarterback*), but confirming and building upon these talents is exceedingly important in determining the way in which you conduct yourself and expand your potential from this point forward. If you indeed are near the top of your class or have represented yourself and your school well on the playing field, this is not bragging; it is fact. Of course, there is a way to go about it and a way not to go about it: *I have been the varsity quarterback since my sophomore year, and after a lot of hard work and close games, our team took the Division title last year,* opposed to *I beat everyone out in my sophomore year and have thrown more game-winning passes than Coach said anybody else at my school has ever done.*

Similarly, but from the opposite angle, you might be hesitant to admit to what you perceive — or rightfully know — as being your weaknesses. I have already admitted to a woeful aptitude for mathematics (believe it or not, I once actually broke down and cried in a college developmental algebra class because I just did not get it), but I have learned over the course of time that one particular flaw is more than offset by different other abilities, and many weaknesses are offset by many strengths. The only faults of which you should feel any "shame" are those over which you have some control, but this is not a book of morality, so I will not waste time going into that.

What you truly do have to know at this stage of your development and looking ahead to college is that it is your responsibility to recognize your abilities and admit to your flaws and thus make your educational plans accordingly. Take note that strengths and weaknesses do not necessarily have to stand apart from each other; there can be a commingling of the two. For example, you might recognize that you are quite skilled in the sciences from an academic standpoint, but you are also interested in creative alternatives that, despite having demonstrated a lesser aptitude, you find more interesting.

This is the sort of dilemma that only you can answer for yourself, but bear in mind that your education plans will go more smoothly if you play to your assets, and your choices are not always limited to either/or. You can apply to colleges and universities that will best accommodate these creative interests along with offering a top-notch education in science. To summarize, selecting a major that does not suit your academic strengths is not the most feasible option for you to pursue with the hope of a successful outcome. This is not to say if it is your dream to let it go, but rather to possibly research a little deeper into other courses that might suit your academic abilities a little better with the outcome of a different major that may fit your own personality even better.

After your period of personal reflection has revealed some insight, you may want to examine how your personal strengths and weaknesses will be reflected in the college environment and if your expectations are realistic or elevated. If these expectations are grandiose (for example, attending Harvard University with a 2.5 GPA), you may need to readjust them to develop a more practical strategy to achieve your goals. This is by no means a failure in your efforts or in the planning process. Let's be real: some of us are more intelligent or capable in certain areas than others, and you must examine what types of gifts you have, and what they can bring to the collegiate table.

For some students, Ivy League is the only sensible option; for others, a community college or a state public university, or even a vocational or technical school will best suit their needs. The thing to realize is that as far as society is concerned, the abilities learned in all ranges of educational institutions are equally important; yet, as far as you are concerned, the "importance" of your area of study and own priorities must be considered on a personal basis. After realistically examining these, it is likely that you will be able to define the best course of action for pursuing the college experience that best fits your personal needs. The beginning of this case study is a good example:

CASE STUDY:
AN UNCERTAIN
STUDENT'S DILEMMA

After a sub-par performance in high school, I was really worried about going to college but knew that I had to do it — and in spite of being worried, I really wanted to do it. After thinking about it for about six months, I sent applications to Wright State University (Dayton, OH), the University of Cincinnati, and the College of Mount St. Joseph, a private institution on Cincinnati's west side.

I selected these schools because of their proximity to my home. More specifically, I chose to apply to Mt. St. Joseph because of the scholarship they offered me to play on their soccer team. But when I weighed everything, "the Mount" is a little hard to get to from where I live, and their academic expectations would be fairly high. The University of Cincinnati is easily accessible from home, but almost "too close," and the area's pretty congested, so my final choice in an educational institution was Wright State, because it gave me enough distance to be independent and start a new life while still being close enough to family and friends.

—Pam Lasko, Student, Wright State University

I will address more of Pam's study again in a later chapter, but the introduction to her story illustrates her immediate needs, beginning with the fact that she took the time to reflect on just what would work for her — and she was honest with herself. She knew her high school grades were unimpressive, and that she in reality did not want to leave the basic geographic location of her hometown. An excellent soccer player, she was tempted by the offer of a scholarship, but was also realistically concerned about the academic expectations in a private institution that also would have required long hours in city rush-hour commute traffic. The University of Cincinnati, like most major colleges today, is notorious for lack of parking and is in an extremely crowded area of town; although geographically closest, the inconvenience and hassle of an overcrowded campus did not appeal to someone who was already leery of attending college. Pam's final choice, despite being farthest away from home in actual mileage, was a relatively "straight shot" up I-75, and also allowed her some breathing room even while still enjoying the security of being at home. Another reality is, that if you win a scholarship for a sport, you need to be prepared for a strong commitment to it and the three to five hours per day for conditioning and practices, not to mention the games. All this time will be taken away from your academics, so you must be sure that you love and will be dedicated to that particular sport. Otherwise, it is not worth doing.

And, while we are on the subject of "home," it should be unequivocally stated that going to college should be your choice, just as which college to attend should be also (bearing in mind, of course, the realities we have already discussed and some that will be later addressed). Nevertheless, your parents should play a part in helping you make your decision, and admittedly there can be some differences between your desires and theirs. The key here, and to avoid any unnecessary unpleasantries, is to include them, if possible, as you begin your reflection. Plus, somewhere along the way, do not forget to give some thought to these two additional questions:

- Are there any familial expectations of me regarding college? Can I satisfy, or do I truly want or need to satisfy, those expectations?
- Do I want to go to college, or is that just something that my family wants me to do?
- Can I pay for this on my own if my parents disagree or cannot afford to financially assist me?

As in the original group at the beginning of this chapter, there in reality is no one but yourself who can answer those questions. "Following in Daddy's footsteps" might appeal to some students, and it may be what you truly want to do, but if the shoes do not fit, and your educational-desire feet are of a different size, you are likely to end up tripping if you try to force yourself to follow his trail. Similarly, if the only reason you intend to go to college is because you have been convinced/coerced/forced by well-intentioned parents and relatives to do so, you are not likely to do well, and may up failing or even dropping out, thus causing a deep resentment between everyone. But once again, the key to avoiding disharmony is to communicate, communicate, communicate. And for the purposes of this book, I am going forward with the assumption that, yes, you want to go to college and for your own reasons, and you are inviting your parents to join in the conversation.

Now, college decisions are not generally the types that are made in a single sit-down parent-child powwow or bull session. By sharing the self-reflection process with your parents, you are inviting their trust by presenting your own. By "sharing," I do not mean revealing your deep-down innermost secrets to your folks, but assuring them that you are giving serious thought before making any such verdict. If they know you are making a conscientious choice, they are much more likely to be amenable to your decisions — whatever they may be.

Let's take a hypothetical example: Recall tailgating Uncle Joe from the Introduction? If, during your self-reflection, you mention to your parents that you might like to major in public administration, and that Ohio State's John Glenn School of Public Affairs curriculum appeals to you, they are not as likely to challenge your decision if that is the course you eventually take. Yet, if you have not given them any idea whatsoever as to your possible leanings, they might (and quite understandably) frown upon thinking that Uncle Joe's slightly inebriated after-Christmas dinner remark is the reason you ask to apply there. There are also some parental problems with college choices for some parents, as they feel that because a particular college was their alma mater, their child must attend as well. This is just another example of why you need to present yourself with a well thought out decision for attending your selections.

Truly, for both yourself and those whose advice you might seek, this self-reflection is also an important indicator of the level-headedness you possess as you move forward with your education. A disciplined self-assessment can only help to plead your case should any controversy should arise. Uncle Joe notwithstanding, let's say you have decided that public administration is truly not your interest after all; you have decided, instead, to pursue a degree in theatre arts — yet, your parents or guardians, who will be providing financial assistance, might have other ideas.

It is critical that you develop a strategy for the college selection process that is for you and you alone, and not for your parents or your friends. Your decision to take a less-profitable course and to attend a smaller college or university because of their distinguished theatre arts program may not be the same choice that your parents want for you, but it is your responsibility to tell them what you want out of the college experience, not vice versa. You are the main part of the equation, not your parents, and it is important to let them know that although you appreciate their love, support, and guidance, you need to make this key decision on your own. If you cannot maintain a sense of control over this, it may be extremely difficult to remain satisfied with that choice and to succeed in your college aspirations. Again, if your decision has been made after some lengthy contemplation, despite any parental concerns, you are more likely to meet with less resistance from them. If your parents are still adamant about where you should or should not go or your choice of major, you may have to alter your plans a bit, especially if you cannot afford to fund a particular school on your own or with scholarships (private schools as well as Ivy League are extremely high in costs). You will only be offered so much in governmental loans as a student (as the amount will depend on your parents income, not yours), and many financial aid offices offer parental loans, but your parents may either refuse them or may not be able to afford it. There are private loans, but they come with a high interest rate, especially if parents do not co-sign, and many times you have to pay on them while in college. Your best path may be to apply to the more affordable community or junior college nearest to you for the first two years. Then when it is time to transfer to that more expensive college that you either need to attend or are determined to attend, you will have more time to apply for more scholarships, and your loans will be cut in half. It will also give your parents more time to see that you are really dedicated to your career plans. Hopefully, this will not be the problem for most of you.

Finally, once you have decided the course of study that works for you, please do not be afraid to seek help and assistance whenever necessary to help you through the application process. Although personal reflection will help you make the appropriate evaluation regarding college, you should not do this based solely on the self-assessment, since there are many unforeseeable obstacles along the way that could hinder your progress in one way or another. Seek the help and advice of more life-experienced people such as parents, teachers, guidance counselors, older siblings, friends, or students you may know who are already attending college to develop a college application and admission strategy that will lead to one of the most satisfying and rewarding experiences that life has to offer. You are more likely to succeed in your college aspirations when you understand and accept the challenges that you are up against while also gaining the support and encouragement of your loved ones and friends.

The following case study is a good example of how the combination of personal choice and the support of others helped one student make her college decision. This study also introduces the concept of writing an application essay, which will be discussed at length later on.

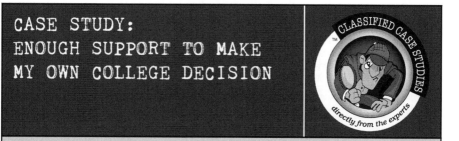

CASE STUDY: ENOUGH SUPPORT TO MAKE MY OWN COLLEGE DECISION

As a senior in high school facing the college application process, I was required to write a personal statement (letter of intent) to be included with the application paperwork. At the age of 17, considering my goals and future intentions was a fairly overwhelming concern. To avoid nervousness, I first approached this statement with the hope of appearing mature and goal-oriented, and not just a teenager looking to party in college.

When starting this statement, I first looked for the support and advice of my parents. Having influenced me to be responsible and build my future goals, my parents were probably the best help I could have hoped for. With their advice, I began my statement with a very brief biographical introduction. The university would get everything they needed from my transcripts and test scores, and did not need to know my life story. I then figured it would be most important to express my intent to take my education seriously, and what goals I hoped to accomplish through the acquisition of a degree.

So, after my brief introduction, I pointed my statement directly into my intended major, which was biology. I then directed my statement to the goals I hoped to achieve from this major and my hope to attend medical school upon graduation. I believed that in focusing on my future goals and the intentions I held for my college education, the university would see me as a student, rather than simply an applicant.

Again, I must say that I had my parents to thank for helping me focus on the future and what I wanted to get out of my education, and I recommend that anyone writing a letter of intent or personal statement of this kind request the advice of a parent or other adult whom you respect and trust.

—Sara McIntosh, Quality Assurance Editor, Convergys

SaraMac (as her friends call her) did attend the college of her first choice (The University of Alabama) and is currently majoring in English at Xavier University in Cincinnati — so much for biology. But the point is that she approached her college aspirations with a solid belief in her abilities and what she wanted to pursue that was well supported by her parents — mainly because she had communicated with them on a steady basis and let them know her intentions.

Of course, SaraMac's case is illustrative, but not unique. One of the reasons Pam Lasko's college career has been successful is that she also had tremendous support from her parents and also three older siblings who had already gone or were still attending college. Although determined to make her own choice, she did not hesitate to ask them their opinions, and at times, almost certainly drove them to distraction with questions — but the fact is that it was obvious to all that she was taking the decision of college very seriously. Pam's story, like Sara's, is especially germane to this chapter because it shows a genuine maturity in self-reflection when it came to selecting a college. She knew that she would never be Harvard material, that sports would interfere with trying to do well in a more challenging environment, and also that it would not be in her best interest (financially or otherwise) to go too far away from home. So, "is college the right choice for Pam?" Based on the above, it certainly is. (Even Mrs. G would have said so.)

The period of self-reflection and an honest assessment of who you are and where you want to go in life are vital for your college aspirations. You have examined your life's history and have recognized your strengths and admitted your weaknesses. These factors have made you who you are today, and they also demonstrate the degree of preparedness that you possess towards the college experience. Your personal characteristics and some of the choices you have already made in your young life may have prepared you quite well for this next path of your life, while others may have led you astray. Where you are emotionally, scholastically, socially, and physically at this stage will play an important role in how you conduct your life from this point forward. If college is in your future, you should start preparing yourself sooner, rather than later, for what is to come, including the application process.

The serious nature of college admissions may be extremely daunting. Though, with a well-established support system in your corner, you will find that the journey that you are about to embark upon may be more fun and even more exciting than you ever imagined. As a human being, you will be weak in some ways and strong in others, but regardless, with perseverance and motivation, you are likely to succeed. The next three chapters will provide a summary of the steps that are required to gain successful admission to the college or colleges of your choice.

Chapter 2

What College Will Best Suit You?

ear Abby:

Help! I have decided to go to college, and these are some of the initial questions that my teachers and counselors have said I should consider. I hear you are good at giving advice. What do you think?

—Signed, Confused

- Do you want to stay near your hometown or go far away to college (and can you afford to go away)?
- Which colleges are most appealing to you?
- Which colleges are in your price range?
- Which colleges provide scholarship opportunities?
- Which colleges have the best programs in your field of interest?
- If you are undecided on a major, which colleges provide the best all-around academic, social, and extracurricular experiences for you?

All right, we have determined that college *is the right choice* for you, and you have made an educational decision that will remain with you for the rest of your life. On the immediate agenda, though, know that for at least the next two to four years, you will be engulfed in books, papers, assignments, and other activities that will play a major role in your young adulthood. Now, the all-pervasive *How do you decide where to go?* dilemma looms large. To answer this extremely important question, you must again examine the results of your personal reflection, as was discussed at length in Chapter 1. This in-depth thinking will enable you to determine the type of academic program you wish to enter and also the overall characteristics that you deem most worthwhile in the college experience. From this point forward, all options presented to you, although borne of more "external" considerations, should be evaluated based on that critical self-examination.

As in the *Is college the right choice for you?* query, the base question *Where do you go?* leads to many more. As we begin to address them, it is important to note that there is no universal order of importance; actually, one student's concerns may not have even crossed another's mind. It is up to you to decide what matters most and to what level of importance you assign each issue. Lists are helpful; they put things into a visual perspective identifying and ranking these criteria in the order in which they are most important to you. For example, take a look at the first question on the list above:

☞ *Do you want to stay near your hometown or go far away to college?*

Although many high school students cannot wait to leave the proverbial nest for treetops unknown, the fact is that some, for the reason of limited financial resources or familial obligations, may not even consider leaving. Conversely, if a student in reality wants to attend an out-of-state college because it meets his or her exact needs (and no local institutions offer a similar program), there may be no choice but to leave. There are even more questions besides those listed above, but for the moment, let's stay with these. Again, there is no set order of importance, but it might be helpful for you to immediately disregard any that may not be significant to you. Discarding unnecessary issues (assuming there are any in this process) will help you better focus on the ones that truly do matter.

Again, let's take the go-away/stay-home dilemma: if one or the other is the definitive answer, well, there you are — that decision has been made. Conversely, if both options are open, the go/stay issue becomes secondary; you can concentrate on the other questions without having to check and see if your local schools offer your chosen course. One word of advice — and admittedly it is much easier said than done — is not to belabor any decisions that can easily be answered or eliminated. For example, let's say your local university has the program you are looking for. It is rated incredibly high in academic circles, and you already know your parents have said they simply cannot afford to send you anywhere (with most state colleges, living can actually cost more than tuition) … do not waste time daydreaming or fancying what "might have been." Be realistic and understand that sometimes the first door will open on to other eventualities; if you start well in your local school, who knows where you might end up?

And, even if leaving town is the option, you can still never be sure where the local/out-of-town university will lead, as was evidenced by one case study in the previous chapter and is reinforced here by a Nashville, Tennessee native's story:

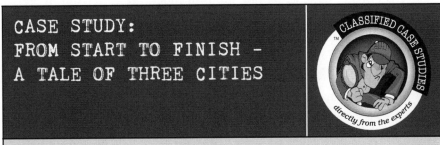

CASE STUDY:
FROM START TO FINISH –
A TALE OF THREE CITIES

When I was in high school, Vanderbilt University was almost within walking distance of my home, and it offered great programs, but I instead chose an elite women's college in the south, Sophie Newcomb of Tulane University, near New Orleans, Louisiana. After a year, I transferred to a school with a more down-to-earth diverse student population, Ohio University in Athens, Ohio. There I earned a Bachelor of Arts Degree in Psychology and positioned myself to offer semi-professional therapy to my "spoon-fed," "lost" and "need-to-find-myself" peers.

During the summer following my second year at Ohio University, I found out that I could earn more credits toward my degree by taking some courses at Vanderbilt. I went home for the summer, took the courses, and then returned to Athens.

After graduating with a BA, I discovered that my career opportunities would broaden with an advanced degree, so I again headed south to Tulane University and earned a master's degree in social work. My first "real job" after graduation was Instructor in Clinical Social Work with the Medical School at the University of Cincinnati.

—Joan S. Lasko, M.S.W.

So, as you can see, the geographically chartered college course you have mapped may lead in directions you never expect — including back home, even if only temporarily.

In quick summary of the local-or-not question, just take note that where you begin your course of study may not be the same institution from which you graduate. The important thing is to get your education underway, do well, and see what develops from there. Believe me; applying to the local college is not the same as signing a bill of indenture to remain in eternal servitude to your hometown. Also, if you cannot attend your first pick of schools because of academics, you have will another fresh chance to improve your grades for acceptance if you transfer with a two year degree in good standing.

Let's examine the other questions — again, bearing in mind that there is no set order of importance that applies to everyone.

☞ *Which colleges are most appealing to you?*

The two most important words are at the end: what kind of college appeals to you? Of primary consideration, of course, is whether the college suits your academic-pursuit desires. Personally speaking (and with all due modesty), I might have been admitted to the all-female Hollins Academy in Virginia with its fine writing courses, but I seriously doubt if the Massachusetts Institute of Technology would even have let me look at their campus from across the street. And even if they had, I truly doubt that I would have been happy, or comfortable, there amongst all the scientists and math-heads.

Aside from academics: are you big on college athletics, either as a participant or fan? You almost certainly would not want to go to a small college with only a few intramural sports; you want more action on the field and court. On the other hand, if you are of a more studious nature and in actuality do not care for athletics, the continual noise and hype and sports partying that goes with a Big Ten school could set your nerves on edge. You may find yourself drowning in an uproarious sea of school colors and wondering how in the world you ended up here when everybody else seems to know all the players' names and virtually ostracize or poke fun at you because you do not.

Other considerations might be geographic climate and your personal preference for natural amenities like beaches or mountains. If you are a Dade County, Florida quarterback, for example, you might not be too successful playing on the windswept University of North Dakota campus. Do you find extreme heat or cold unbearable? Are you easily depressed by too many cloudy, rainy days? The exact nature of your studies (for example, marine biology or forestry) may dictate that certain locales are essential, so you truly must ensure that you will be comfortable in the surroundings.

And what about the town closest to the college? In the case study above, Ms. Lasko was happy to be so close to New Orleans and its colorful French Quarter and endless seafood bounty, but a student with whom I attended grad school once told me he left Tulane because he could not stand all the noise and the oppressive heat — plus, he was allergic to seafood. And while thinking about the town, you might also want to consider more practical issues, such the possibilities of part-time employment. What kind of opportunities are there for a student who wants to "earn as they learn?" Does the town offer a good, clean, and safe environment?

— Or, do any of the above questions not truly matter to you?

Again, here is a good place for you to start eliminating some options. Unless there is a strong, compelling reason to consider a college that initially does not appeal to you, do not waste time on it. What do I mean by "compelling?" Let's say you are that Florida football player, and you are offered a full-ride scholarship to UND — you may have to seriously consider buying some heavy clothing and heading north. Realistically speaking, though, the fact is that you are likely to spend the better part of the next two to four years in the college's environment, so make sure you take everything into consideration if you find yourself toying with the idea of going somewhere you would not otherwise have found desirable.

Bear in mind, you must evaluate the most important preferences in determining which college or university is most attractive and appealing to you. These may include, along with what we have already discussed, classroom size, teacher-to-student ratio, and other non-athletic extracurricular activities. Are you interested in the "Greek" life (sororities and fraternities)? Are you interested in working on a school's newspaper or participating on debate teams? Are you looking for clubs that make a difference in the community? Are you looking for organizations that relate to your major? It also goes without elaboration that there are most likely other considerations unique to you, and you should seriously examine them without feeling silly or embarrassed; their importance is yours alone to evaluate.

You also need to actually visit the college and its campus yourself. You cannot get the "feel" of a college from books or virtual online views. You need to go there and see it. I have had friends set on one particular college their entire life, then they went on a college tour at another school and fell in love with that school and never looked back at their lifelong dream. Each school has its own atmosphere and personality, and they don't suit everyone.

One more question to consider when researching and deciding upon a college, is what type of internships do they offer? Although not every degree requires internships, the ones that do will make a world of difference. Many students are hired after college because of the connection or impression they made while interning. Some of the less notable colleges have better internship programs then you would realize. One of my friends obtained an "athletic" scholarship at a very prestigious (and expensive) private college. Most of these "athletic" scholarships will fall under "academic" scholarships. Unfortunately, he had too good of a time while attending school, and he failed a few of his classes and lost his "academic" scholarship. The tuition was too high for him to pay, and he had to return home to a local state school. The irony is that this state school just happened to have a fantastic internship program for his major, and because of the contacts he made interning, he is now an extremely successful and financially wealthy businessman.

☞ *Which colleges are in your price range?*

Before addressing the meat of this topic, let's talk about your intended professional goals. Now that you have made the decision to attend college, you must decide if you wish to pursue an associate's or bachelor's degree. For many majors, including nursing, an associate's degree may be all that is required to earn the desired position and expand the potential for strong earning power within that particular job market. For other programs or majors, a bachelor's degree or higher may be required, and therefore the emphasis should be on four-year colleges or universities that provide these offerings. Naturally, the difference in cost is significant; yet, as you will see in a minute, for the most part, the two-year associate programs can be applied to eventual bachelor's work; as in that Associates Nursing degree (Registered Nurse), once earned, can be developed into a Bachelor of Nursing degree with only an extra year and a half more of courses.

So, now let's consider your price range. With the cost of college tuition rising on an annual basis, this is perhaps one of the most critical questions to consider when making the decision of which college to attend. How much is tuition going to cost? If you are going away, what about the price of room and board? Are these affordable, and, if you cannot finance them on your own, what types of grants, scholarships, and loans are available? You may possess the academic credentials and the wherewithal to attend an Ivy League university, but without the appropriate level of financing, your dream may not be realized without serious financial difficulty. Unfortunately, many colleges and universities, particularly those categorized as private, are often unaffordable to an extreme degree, with tuition and room and board topping the $40,000 and higher per year mark. However, the Ivy League universities frown upon loans, and if you have financial need, they will help fund your education without all of those endless loans. It is something to look into with the private colleges as well. It does not hurt to let them know that you are interested, but that you do not want to go deep into debt. Many

times they can come up with more money if they really want you to attend. It never hurts to try. Just be realistic and know that you will need a more affordable back-up college if they cannot come up with the needed funds.

But private colleges are not the only academic environments that create financing problems for students. The costs of state-funded colleges and universities also continue to skyrocket, and with the cost of the rising tuition, room and board, books and other fees, the total amount is still not affordable without you and perhaps your parents going deeply into debt. Even many universities that offer online programs charge high tuition rates that are difficult for many students to manage.

For some, the best way to begin a college education may be to attend a local two-year community college, where the tuition rates are much more affordable. Another huge benefit in attending a community college first where students can remain in the home environment is that it eliminates room and board rates, which are usually quite a bit more than the tuition. Also, the majority of credits can transfer to four-year colleges or universities in future years. It serves a purpose in other ways as well. If you are not positive of your major, it gives you time to investigate other paths as well and it is a stepping stone in difficulty of classes from high school to four year colleges. Community colleges have smaller classes and therefore the professors usually have more one-on-one time for any student who may need it. Their classes range from 20-30 students, whereas most universities range from 100-500 students per class for introductory courses. Many community colleges have honors programs, which if you are accepted, is something that will help you gain easier acceptance into a larger university or college that you might not have gotten into straight from high school. For many students, and more precisely their parents, the cost of a college education is alarming, and therefore these issues must be seriously considered in the earliest stages of the college admission process.

I do not want to get into the question of student loans; there are far too many complexities and options beyond my expertise to be considered that I cannot even begin to address. Suffice it to say that I am currently paying on my own, and I have met others who are still paying on their loans 20-30 years later, and that is about as close as I can come to any "first-hand knowledge" on the matter, except to impart to you to try to stay away from loans as much as possible. Though, I must share one further thought before moving on:

When, after a long absence, I decided to return to college and finish my degree, I applied to three local schools, two private and one state-run. In my particular case, the private school I ended up attending, Xavier University (XU), accepted more incoming credits than either the College of Mount St. Joseph or the University of Cincinnati would have done. Therefore, XU's higher cost was offset, and I was able to finish my Bachelor of Arts (English) much sooner and move on to graduate school at that same institution. I still paid more in undergraduate tuition, but in balancing out all the factors (less time is also less room and board), XU was the better choice for me. Plus, because of my success as an undergraduate, I was able to hold four graduate assistant positions that greatly reduced the cost of my Master of Arts (MA/English) studies. Although this situation was awfully different from someone just coming out of high school, the moral of this story is that you do need to see if there may be a good reason to pay more to a private institution to meet your own particular goals and requirements.

☞ *Which colleges provide scholarship opportunities?*

When considering your college of choice, think about whether you possess a specific skill or talent that will enable you to obtain a grant or scholarship to offset the costs of tuition. This also demonstrates the importance of maximizing academic performance at the earliest possible time to improve the chances of obtaining scholarships. You cannot even imagine how many different scholarships are available to students today. Some colleges have automatic scholarships for incoming freshmen, if your grades and test scores (SAT/ACT) meet the criteria, and many of these are renewable for up to your bachelor's degree. Other scholarships are based upon a wide variety of criteria, including those related to cultural background, gender, extracurricular activities, community service, financial need, leadership skills, and other talents that students may possess. Therefore, it is important to determine if scholarships are an option, depending upon your personal situation, and to seek as many scholarship opportunities as possible if you fit the designated criteria. There are also private scholarships (sometimes under "foundation" scholarships) that are for that particular college only, but are from private benefactors. These are one that you will need to search for beyond the colleges' own website.

Please note that there are an abundance of scholarships that can apply to any institution just as others are offered exclusively to one school. High school counselors often have good leads on what scholarships are available (and if they are not that informative, then contact your local school board for more help), and in this present day, there is more than enough information readily available on the web, a good "beginning sampler" of which is included at the end of this book, in Appendix I.

One thing to remember though is that the scholarships you find on the web are usually nationwide. Even though they are worth more money, you actually have a much better chance at the local ones, as there is less competition. Many of national scholarships have thousands of applications. I actually received a denial-reply back from one telling me that 80,000 others had also applied.

Which colleges have the best programs in your field of interest?

How do you know which colleges or universities offer a major in your field of interest? The answer is simple: research. Again, counselors and the internet will prove invaluable. You must address your options through a personalized research endeavor that will enable you to single out those colleges and universities that fit your specific criteria, especially those related to your major or field of study. If you do not fully research your options, you may find yourself without a clear vision regarding your college education. You must examine your options thoroughly and without reservation to make educated choices for your future schooling. If your major or interest is biology, then you might want to pursue those colleges that offer strong biology programs, or if you prefer accounting, you might consider schools that offer highly competitive business courses. Even if a particular school meets all your needs so far as climate, location, extracurriculars, and such, it does not make sense to attend a college or university that is strong in artistic studies when your major is pre-med. I cannot stress this enough: thoroughly researching your course options is critical to make the best possible selection. It will also help to research their career placement rates; such as how many students find jobs in their field upon graduation and, as I stated before, their internship options.

If you are undecided on a field of interest, which colleges provide the best all-around academic and extracurricular experiences?

It is no surprise that many students find themselves in a position of uncertainty regarding a field of interest, and therefore they enter the college application process with an undecided major. There is nothing wrong with this scenario. Even though you have self-reflected and given much consideration, you may still be unsure where your true college-related talents and strengths lie, and you may therefore be confused regarding choices. Please do not get discouraged, as being "undecided" is not the end of the world. Bear in mind that roughly half of your college classes will be what are known as "core" — in other words, they are required of everyone, regardless of the eventually-chosen major. Many students begin college by taking these core courses and find themselves developing new interests, learning their strengths, and shaping their eventual decision on a major even as they complete the required course load.

Even for those who think that they are set on one particular major may change their minds once in college, just as those who are not decided will

be making up their minds. A variety of things can influence you to change your chosen path. It could be the difficulty of the classes required (not everyone is cut out to be a doctor), or perhaps you hate the courses that pertain to your major (if this is the case, then that particular major might just not be for you), or perhaps you had your heart set on a career that is highly competitive and you can't handle it, or you do not want to move across the country in order to obtain a job. Perhaps you cannot achieve the test scores needed to get into medical or law schools. You just might find another choice more to your liking or more interesting than you thought. Whatever the reason, when researching colleges, it does not hurt to see what other majors they offer that just might appeal to you as well.

In addition, as you work toward deciding upon a major or field of study, consider what else the school has to offer. Again, return to the list you made (location, cost, climate, extracurriculars, and such) outlining your preferences in the order of importance; this should help you in weighing all the factors according to their value. You must ultimately determine the balance that is best for you, and then seek a college or university that will expand your breadth of knowledge and experience in the best possible manner.

The moment that you begin to take the college application process seriously, you should begin the necessary research. You are likely to find that you are more than prepared for the challenges that await you after you have made that critical first selection of a few colleges or universities that you find most appealing. As the ancient Chinese proverb says, "The journey of 1,000 miles begins with one step," and that first step will always be the hardest because you know there are still so many more to go ... but you also will never get anywhere without putting one foot in front of the other.

When you have made these initial selections, call or email the specific colleges to request more information. If you do know your major, try calling into that department and talking to someone who can tell you what you might need to get into that program. Also start asking questions of your teachers, counselors, parents, and other acquaintances. What do they know about these colleges? What is their reputation? Do they know anyone who has attended these colleges? If so, what were their experiences? Would they recommend these colleges to you? Are they a good fit? What else can they tell you about them? How easy is it set up a tour? If you do not ask these questions, then you may never get the answers that you need to make an informed decision, and therefore, you may make a wrong choice that could have been avoided.

A word of caution: While it is helpful to seek others' personal opinions as described above, bear in mind that your goals and the things you look for may not be the same as theirs. Again, let's take Uncle Joe: his memories of Ohio State (assuming he *can* recall anything, after all those tailgate parties) are obviously fond, but if you are wanting to attend because of the John Glenn College of Public Affairs, Joe's experiences may not in actuality apply to you — and also do not forget the age difference. Things today at THE Ohio State University may be a far cry from what he recalls. Along the same-but-different lines, you have no doubt heard the expression that "One man's trash is another man's treasure." The same is true here. Joe's fond memories may be offset by someone else's intense dislike for the institution. Ask questions, listen to the answers, but do not go strictly by what others say — either negative or positive — because even the most well-meaning of them might mislead you. And once again, I can never say it enough; make a visit to these colleges if at all possible. Then take all of these factors into consideration.

Yes, by all means ask as many people and solicit as much personal information as you can, but ultimately — again — this is your decision to make. Look online, request brochures, and keep your own agenda in mind. Review the materials you requested from various colleges as much as possible. Not only will these materials provide you with physical descriptions of the college campuses, they will also enable you to determine if the key characteristics of those schools align with your specific needs. A single glimpse at one of these books may be the deciding factor in selecting a college or university. In this day and age, however, not all colleges use the paper trail as much when most of the information is found on their website. But in this you need to be patient and search for the answers, as I have found that many schools websites are not as user friendly as they should be. The information is there, but some websites take longer to find your answers. If you get frustrated, leave the computer and come back at a later time and start again.

The questions that have been raised in this chapter provide a glimpse into the various criteria that should be evaluated in your effort to identify colleges and universities that best suit your needs. There are a number of important factors to prepare for when applying for colleges, and one simple task should help you discover a wealth of information that will help you make the most informed choice: research. Without this critical step, it may be extremely difficult to identify the school or schools that are most feasible to you, and research prevents ignorance from replacing intelligence and knowledge. These two characteristics are essential in making a successful decision that will forever influence your life in a positive manner.

You should always have a couple of back up colleges as well for the "just in case" factor; "just in case" your test scores or grades are not high enough for acceptance, or "just in case" you are not accepted for some other reason that may never be explained (which has happened to a couple of my friends), or "just in case" you cannot afford to go to your first choice.

ear Confused:

Assuming you have read through this chapter (which is my first piece of advice) and have made a list or lists and thought things over, the next thing you should do is send for more information on the schools that may have caught your interest. This is by no means the end-all final list, but it is a good place to start. I know it all seems overwhelming, but the more you look into this, the clearer the picture will become. Good luck.

—Abby

Chapter 3

How Do You Begin to Prepare for College?

The college experience is frightening, intimidating, overwhelming, exciting, fun, and rewarding all rolled up into one. But before you can even begin to experience any or all of these on campus, you must be prepared for the tasks that await you in developing a feasible yet worthwhile college admissions plan that will enable you to gain acceptance to that campus. Do not despair; if you have gotten this far along in the book, you have obviously laid the most important groundwork (self-reflection) and foundation (deciding upon the best type of college for you) for building your collegiate future. You are also willing to continue reading, at least for now — and that is a solid indicator of your potential college success.

Along the lines of despair, do not waste valuable time (or fingernail-biting) worrying if you truly do have the ability to succeed in college, reading this book notwithstanding. Given the wide variety of higher-educational institutions proliferating throughout our country, there is a college or vocational

institution that suits almost every person with higher-education aspirations. With very few exceptions, everyone, if he or she truly wants it, can succeed in college.

Let's briefly pause here. Just what do you consider *success*? Some students would consider themselves successful for getting by with the minimum GPA (grade point average) required to receive a diploma. Other students, of course, hold success and achievement to a higher GPA standard. Then there are students who do not measure their success by GPA; perhaps some of the work they have done while attending college has led to an excellent job opportunity immediately after the graduation ceremony, or they have been offered a chance to continue their education at the next level. So, although there are certainly some preconceived ideas about the meaning of the word, the bottom line is that you — and you alone — know what you would consider as being successful. And you should know the reasonable expectations to set for yourself to achieve your idea of success and achievement.

It should also be mentioned that even within immediate families, the idea of success and achievement is unique to each individual student. While we have all heard the horror stories of siblings or cousins being matched or pitted against each other for parental expectations or bragging rights, only the student can decide his or her own definition of success and strive accordingly. Furthermore, as the years have passed, the ideas of higher education and life accomplishment have become more intertwined that college is almost a necessity by now — but the difference in students and their concepts of success remains distinctly unique. The following case study is a good example.

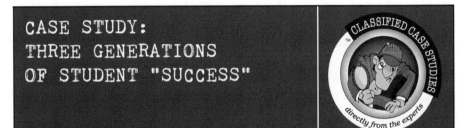

CASE STUDY: THREE GENERATIONS OF STUDENT "SUCCESS"

I was born in 1935, the youngest of three — and by eight years. My older brother enlisted in the United States Marine Corps during WWII, and my older sister took secretarial/stenographer classes and co-oped during high school. My brother survived the war and went on to a lifelong career with the United States Army Corps of Engineers and General Services Administration; my sister found steady employment and was paid well (considering the era and the fact she was a woman). None of us went to college at the "normal" age, but we were all "successful."

Later on, after marrying and raising two sons, I felt the urge to take some higher-level classes. When I filled out an application for college, the most difficult part was bridging the gap of the 25 years since I had been graduated from high school. Since this was a two-year school, I do not remember that the requirements were too stringent in the composition department. However, I was able to test out of Freshman English I, II, and III by taking a placement test and scoring in the 97th percentile. The biggest section of that all-day test was written English, including composition, spelling, and grammar.

I eventually earned an associate degree in library science, but my career position was as a church administrative assistant, where my writing skills were of utmost importance. Most of the letters signed by my supervisor were actually composed by me. Now retired, I presently staff a homework room for intermediate-grade students and am able to be of considerable help to these youngsters with their grammar, spelling, etc. while also proofreading for a widely circulated monthly Christian periodical, *The Restoration Herald.*

Today's students are not being equipped to write comprehensively. Of my two sons who attended a well-known area college [Miami University of Ohio] in the early 80's, the older one excelled in composition skills and received 4.0 grades in English throughout his college career. The younger had the same English teacher in high school but chose not to avail himself of that ability. Currently, my older son heads up a regional sales division for a major commercial/corporate enterprise. The younger son started working behind the counter at one of the largest fast-food chains during high school and has been a general manager for that corporation for over 20 years now.

Altogether, I have six grandchildren (and one great-grandchild, but she is too young to be thinking even of kindergarten). My oldest grandson was graduated from Cornell University with honors. In chronological order, the next-oldest works for a fraud investigation firm (he has nearly finished his BS in English); the next is a mechanic for an automobile dealership in Nashville TN (he was graduated from a prestigious automotive school in Nashville with a certificate in bodywork); the next is learning the bakery business in a health food chain (he quit school in his senior year but did get a GED). My only granddaughter is currently unemployed, as is her brother — both of whom graduated high school but did not go to college.

—Marilyn Abbott,
Administrative Assistant (ret.) for the Madeira Church of Christ

As is shown by the study, talk about how times have changed. Also, I am sure you have noted that every "older" contributor to the case studies thus far has mentioned how writing skills have declined — but that is not my current concern. What I am trying to demonstrate here is how, in just a couple of generations, college (or quality vocational training) has gone from being virtually unnecessary to almost totally essential to find one's way to success in the world — and that everyone has his or her own idea of what that means.

The most important thing to address at this stage, the beginning of the college application process, is a solid assessment of your expectations to determine if they are in conformance with your idea of success. It goes without saying that the chances of accomplishment rapidly diminish if your expectations are unrealistic: do you in actuality expect to hold a 4.0 GPA overall when you know that math (and its attendant core courses) is going to be a real challenge? Sure, there is no harm in trying, but *trying* and *expecting* are different in that *trying* is realistic but *expecting* is not. Therefore, the first step toward eventual success is to prepare for college realistically. And for that, let's hope you have applied yourself in your past education well enough to be able to take a realistic approach now.

As I discussed in Chapter 1, developing a set of realistic expectations begins with high school. Without these experiences, we would have nothing substantial to build on in college. After all, you will need to process what you learn in high school to move on to the next educational level — just as you needed to process from grade school to middle school and from middle school to high school. Formal education is designed to be a continual process, with each new level building upon the prior level — but the prior level must be solid and sturdy enough to allow for further construction. You would not want to place a load of 5,000 lbs on a platform designed to hold only 4,000 and expect it to hold up, right? This would be unrealistic — and foolish; the entire platform so carefully constructed over the course of 12 years collapses in one moment of an ill-conceived decision.

This chapter will evaluate the various preparation strategies that are required for students who wish to achieve their college dreams and expectations in a realistic fashion. In simplest terms, high school may be viewed as a means to an end; on the other hand, it is also viewed as a significant portion of a teenager's life, one that facilitates growth and knowledge development, and not just in the academic sense of the word. High school is much more than academic performance (including Mrs. G's classroom participation points); it also entails pep rallies, sporting events, proms and homecomings, plays and concerts, and general social interactions with other students and the community, all of which contribute to the learning curve in many important and different ways.

Have you ever stood on a bridge or other high spot that looked over a railroad yard? Think of high school as a vast array of winding social and academic tracks, with switches, semaphores, and side-rails that encourage students to examine and observe in preparation for the Grand Central Station known as college. I refer to this as "Grand Central" because it merges all that was learned and acquired during high school to shape you into who you are today, the "you" who wants to climb aboard the College Express and experience all the scenery along the way as you travel to the destinations you ultimately seek. You are in an important transition period in your life, and you must learn as much as you can from the experience — oh, and be prepared to adapt to change; there will be some unexpected stops and possible delays along the way, but unless you are completely unprepared or unrealistic in your expectations, there should be no train wreck of Casey Jones-ian proportions.

A good way to view this transitional period and make it seem less daunting is to bear in mind that, at least since eighth grade, you have been packing and preparing for this journey; it is time to release the brake and proceed. With any luck, you have packed carefully and made sure to properly fill out the ID tags — in other words, your academic and social skills are in good order.

Let's cut to the chase: yes, elementary/grade school almost automatically prepared you for junior high/middle school, which in turn automatically prepared you for high school, but preparing for college during the high

school years is an ongoing process that requires a significant commitment to positive academic performance. You may be homecoming king and play in every football game, you may be the female lead in every musical, but colleges and universities will almost without exception review academic credentials above all other criteria in the earliest stages of the admission process, and you must therefore maximize your preparation efforts to guarantee successful outcomes. At this high school stage of your life, you cannot do all this alone; your parents are the first source of guidance and help. They know you better than anyone else (perhaps even you, for the moment), and if they have taken a proactive interest in grooming you for college, you are already one step ahead of many other students in that your academic performance has been well-nurtured.

This "nurturing" begins with the selection of the appropriate level and categories of high school coursework from one year to the next — a selection decided by the combined efforts of you and your parents. Stephen Kramer and Michael London address this concept in *The New Rules of College Admissions*, in which the authors stress the importance of open dialoguing between students and their parents to best determine the course choice and level of intensity. Not only does open communication at home facilitate good education, but a student is more likely to be balanced and overall satisfied with the high school experience if the nurturing and parental attention have included his or her input. Dialogue (two speakers), not monologue (one speaker) is the key to solid communication; both you and your parents must be open and honest in this ongoing discussion.

It is critical to gauge how your academic performance progresses from one year to the next; as you grow, you will change, particularly during adolescence. Therefore, it is vital to your eventual success to continually assess your own personal strengths and weaknesses and to monitor how they relate to academic achievement. Your performance will also be watched by teachers and guidance counselors, who should be able to identify patterns in academic execution and also growth or decline in specific subject areas (hence my AP-English and less-complex math of which I spoke in Chapter 1).

For those of you who do not have parental guidance or for those whose parents are just as confused as you, you can still do this without them. You are on the path to being an adult and if your desire is strong enough, you can research all of what I have just said yourself. Many times the students who have the least amount of help, but have the desire to succeed, will do even better. You have already shown that by reading this book and any other research you may be doing. But if you reach a point where you do need adult guidance, there is almost always someone at your school, whether it be a teacher, guidance counselor, principal, or even a secretary, that will be more than willing to give you assistance and to sit down with you and talk over your concerns. Most of the adults working in any school system are there because they care and are happy to help those who are trying to help themselves.

Most importantly, if you are a student with sincere college aspirations, you should remain focused on preparing yourself for college-level coursework through the selection of classes that provide some degree of difficulty and challenge throughout your high school career. Without this type of preparation, you may find yourself trailing behind during the college application process, particularly if you have not demonstrated a clear progression of growth with respect to academic performance. Your best option is to work proactively to discover these talents early so that you will have as many options as possible with respect to advancing academic growth through complex and difficult coursework choices — and yet, even at this stage, you do not want to set unrealistic goals (I never signed up for Pre-Calculus). There is much to be said for developing a college-bound strategy compatible to your academic strengths; they should challenge, yes, push, yes, but not overwhelm. (I was challenged and pushed by even the least-complex math, and quite frankly, barely passed; anything more complicated would have overwhelmed me.)

Sorry; I am still a bit unnerved just thinking about those days, but we are talking about you now. While developing your strategies, you will also discover that your skills may be best suited for specific areas of interest, such as the sciences or artistic expression. The terms "left brain" and "right brain" come to mind, and although all human beings possess a brain and a conscience, we are all wired differently, and therefore we have different strengths and weaknesses. You may be strong in mathematics, while I excel in writing and English, and there is nothing wrong with these differences. Your job is to identify these core abilities and to expand upon them as early as possible in high school to develop a specific strategy for growth that accommodates your ultimate educational goals. Colleges are more and

more looking at the level of the classes you are enrolled in. International Baccalaureate, AICE, Honors, Advanced Placement, and dual enrollment classes of course, carry more weight than the regular "unweighted" classes. But if you take these classes (knowing that they are already difficult for you) and fail, then that will not help you either. As I said before, you need to challenge yourself, just do not push yourself over the edge either.

There is much to be said about achieving good grades throughout the academic career, and although this has already been tagged as primary, there is far more criteria than pure GPA to gaining admission to your college of choice. Let's take a quick glance at this "non-graded" criteria. Throughout high school, it is your responsibility to develop a portfolio that combines academic strengths with extracurricular activities and participation as a member of that community known as your school. Every student forms an integral part of that community — some to a higher and more noticeable (and in a positive sense) degree than others; it behooves you to be one of the more visible and active students in your school. Also, do not neglect the building of social skills and meaningful relationships amongst your teachers and peers; these will also serve a valuable purpose in promoting an effective petition to attend the college you have chosen.

A strong academic record, then, is based upon a clearly defined level of achievement that is earned throughout the high school career and includes both non-GPA and GPA-related factors. Normally, academic grades are earned based upon performance on tests, quizzes, exams, and other required assignments, although class participation may also play a role in determining the final grade. It is a responsible choice to work hard throughout the grading period to obtain grades that are acceptable from a college admission standpoint. How well you perform in an academic setting is entirely up to you, given your existing strengths and weaknesses, and it is ultimately your decision to excel or fail within a given classroom setting or series of assignments.

As a college-bound student, in the classroom and in extracurricular ventures, it is your duty to perform always to the best of your ability. You must ensure that you possess the necessary credentials to gain entrance to the school of your choice. The ability to expand upon existing skills and strengths is one of the most important facets of the high school career, and the continuous advancement of such talents and assets is critical to personal development.

Another requirement as a college-bound student is also to determine how you may further advance your overall standing within the high school setting, and perhaps you are among an elite group of students who possess exemplary academic ability. For these students, consistently strong performance is practically effortless, and they often have a grade advantage over other students — but many of them choose not to participate in classroom discussion or extracurricular activities, or community involvement, which will give you a bit of unexpected leverage in the eyes of an admissions committee.

Other students also have strong academic ability, yet must work tirelessly to advance their own objectives. I fall into this category, and although my high school grades were strong and I was ranked in the top 10 percent of my graduating class, I was frustrated many times by my inability to earn a perfect score on an exam or quiz, even if I had studied for hours on end. You may find yourself in a similar situation, and although it is exasperating, you can gain additional "non-tangible" rewards that might not be observed in a student who excels without any effort — the greatest "non-tangible" being the sense of satisfaction that you overcame a perceived weakness and got that 100 percent. The key here is to not forget, as was said above, to perform to your best ability and to be well-rounded academically and in extracurricular and community-service events. The obvious desire to work hard and participate will, nine times out of 10, put you in better overall standing than that genius who in reality does not need to strain him or herself and (for whatever reason) remains aloof from the rest. This is the "leverage" of which I just spoke.

A consistent effort to develop the best possible high school academic record is particularly important throughout the junior and senior years. Though, the sophomore year has become increasingly noticeable as a transition year for many students who might not have known what to expect in the first year. This is not to say that you are able to slack in your first year or two of high school. You still need to keep up your grades, as they are all averaged together. What I am trying to impart is that you may need to adjust to high school life and also that you might not be able to challenge yourself with a more rigorous course load until after your first year. If you select challenging coursework, the chances are that you will improve your standing with the college or colleges of your choice, as this indicates you are making a concerted effort to demonstrate your acceptance of a demanding course load, which is a necessary requirement in the college environment. A performance of "B" or better in an accelerated or advanced placement (AP) course is likely to gain favorable attention and review from a college admissions committee over a simpler, easier course load where stronger grades were earned. The difference lies in the fact that you are willing to accept courses that are not necessarily easy for you to understand or comprehend, and also that you are willing to take risks in improving your academic credentials with the potential for a higher GPA. These choices are undoubtedly encouraging to colleges and universities, particularly those with low admission-to-applicant ratios. In these cases, advanced or accelerated course selections may almost be required to establish improved academic standing. Another thing to think of is the age-old "senioritis." Just because you have done well and challenged yourself the first three years, does not mean that you can relax and let some of it slide your senior year. You must continue to strive to be your best during this time as well.

Once the decision has been made to pursue a college education, you must also determine how your academic credentials, or lack thereof, will positively or negatively influence a college admissions committee. If you possess a strong academic history, you might believe that you have admission to the college of your choice in the proverbial bag. Not so fast. You might possess stellar grades, but there are other requirements that college admissions committees are looking for that will enable you to apply to the college of your choice and to succeed in your efforts; I have been and will continue to discuss these throughout this book.

Contrary to thinking you are guaranteed acceptance, you may be of the less-optimistic mindset that thinks: *My grades will never be good enough for some colleges or universities, so why bother with any attempts to improve academic performance?* This is a poor attitude to adopt, as it is more important for you to work tirelessly to improve your grades and to establish an acceptable level of academic performance — a most-desirable character trait — that will provide a complimentary glimpse of your true scholarly potential.

If the school of your choice has academic requirements that surpass anything that you can possibly obtain, no matter how hard you work at it, then perhaps that college is just not for you. Or maybe it is not for you at this time. You might do better by attending a community college first, then trying again for that college after you receive your associate degree. A lot can happen in two years, but no matter the outcome, there is always another college out there for you if you truly have the desire to attend.

To paint a metaphorical picture, the movie *Rudy* told the story of a real-life Notre Dame student who had neither the skills nor size nor speed required for college football, but who always gave a 100-percent effort in the practice squad and refused to be discouraged. For this reason alone, Rudy had the undying loyalty of his Fighting Irish teammates, who threatened to walk out unless he was allowed to play in a real game. No one truly could ever have realistically taken him for a football player, but he was beyond doubt a driven, hard-working overachiever, and for that reason, he was taken seriously as a person. If you want to attend college, it is your responsibility to make the effort to be taken seriously, not only as a student but also a person, from a college admissions standpoint, because nobody else will do this for you. As I have said before, you control your destiny, and you must be the one to make your college career dreams come true. Your grades matter, but what might ultimately matter more is the determination you showed to achieve them.

To summarize before moving on, a combination of important factors is essential in developing a successful college admissions portfolio. Your primary responsibility is to determine how to balance academic performance with extracurricular activities, community service, and leadership skills to gain entrance into your college of choice. This is not easy, and it may be extremely difficult for you to remain on task in all of these areas throughout this process of your high school years, but anything is possible if you want it enough. You must dedicate yourself to achieving superior academic performance so that your credentials will support your commitment to college achievement. Although this process is difficult because you will never know the exact criteria that the admissions team is looking for, if you possess a serious and steadfast commitment to gaining college acceptance at the school of your choice, you will be more than ready for a challenge of this nature and magnitude — and it will show. More and more admissions committees are looking at the activities part of the application as well. They want to see that you are a well-rounded individual and that you have become that way through participation in clubs, organizations, sports, and community involvement. They will also see if you join many different organizations for groups. They might also want to know how involved you actually are in these clubs or organizations, as commitment is an important factor in the application process. At the same time, if you have to work many hours, or play several sports, they do realize that you may not have the time to be as well-rounded as others, but it still shows an obligation to above and beyond your academics.

As I have emphasized throughout this chapter, long-term academic performance is critical, and the other important component within this grade-centric criteria that should not be ignored is standardized testing, which I will discuss in the next chapter.

Chapter 4

A Few Words About Standardized Tests

*I*magine yourself in your junior year of high school, enjoying life and your friends as best as you can. Then the inevitable arrives: it is time to take the College Board Standard Assessment Test (SAT) or the American College Testing Program (ACT), and you begin to panic. Your worries may have merit, and you are justifiably nervous regarding what is expected of you. You have most likely taken standardized tests in elementary or middle school, but those tests never meant as much to you as the grown-up high school version. Standardized tests should be taken quite seriously, and you should put your heart and soul into making sure that you do your best when the time comes. The SAT and the ACT are an especially important step towards gaining acceptance into the college or university of your choice, and therefore you must be able to demonstrate that you possess the knowledge and skills necessary to achieve acceptable scores — after you have proven you are not too "chicken" to sign up.

This may come as a shock, but not all people who excel in their academic credentials perform well on standardized tests, and more than a handful of students in reality stress just *thinking* about them, never mind *taking* them. But have heart ... there are some colleges that students may be admitted to based not so much on SAT or ACT scores; but rather, by their GPA and the level of classes they have taken that will more accurately reveal their capabilities. Make no mistake — some institutions will place more emphasis on these standardized scores than will others, and more colleges are starting to lean that way, so you should prepare yourself as best as possible by availing yourself of the preliminary practice tests and any study workshops offered at your high school (such as the PSAT) or online practice. But in the overall scheme of things, you can only prepare yourself as much as possible and (as always) do your absolute best.

Practices and workshops are beneficial, but in a real-life standardized testing situation, how can you possibly know what to anticipate? The old adage "expect the unexpected" might be appropriate in this situation, and even though you might be afraid at the sudden this-is-it feeling, accept the situation for what it is and do your best. You should feel satisfied when you leave the testing center knowing that you have accomplished something important. The key thing to not forget is that although you know *how* you are supposed to perform on standardized tests, there are no real rules to follow as to how to achieve that performance. Are you a student who does better to study up to the last possible minute, or are you one who actually does better by allowing a 24-48 hour "time out" away from studying prior to taking such a test? Standardized test performance largely depends upon your personal and academic ability, and this does not follow any particular set of rules. There is another distinct difference in the two tests that some have found to help some. If you test well in math, then the SAT might be the easier test to take as it is one-third math, one-third verbal, and one-third writing. The ACT is divided into more sections (so less math); math, reading, English, science, and writing. It is best to plan on taking each one; then, if needed, concentrate on the one you did better on.

However, there are a few easier ways to help prepare yourself for these tests. One of the most important would be to answer *every* question, even the ones you do not know (as of March 2016, there is no longer a penalty for guessing on the SAT). When starting one of the sections, first answer all of the questions that you do know, then go over the more difficult ones. Take an educated guess on the ones that you are able to, then right before time is up, Christmas tree (yes, that is what I meant) all of those that you do not know. You have at least a 20 percent chance of being correct, which is still better than 0 percent. One basic rule of thumb is that you should have a better chance of getting more of these "guesses" correct if you use the same letter to answer all of those in that particular section. For example, if you start with "C" (which is supposed to be the universal answer for the unknown), then use "C" all of the way down in that part of the test. A right answer is a right answer whether you guessed or not, so answer every single question!

Something else to think of when taking a standardized test is how you are actually feeling. Get a good night's sleep and stay away from distractions such as disagreements or arguments. Eat a good breakfast and, if you are an early person, go out to breakfast with others also taking the test to help relax you and ease some anxieties. If you are a late riser and hate to eat right away, at least have something on the way there.

Another factor to think about (if you have the option) is where you will actually be taking the test. I have heard students complain about feeling cramped in smaller desks, or freezing in one place where the air was turned down low. To help with the cold, always take a jacket and layer yourself so you can easily remove clothes in case it is too warm. Feeling comfortable is extremely important when taking these type of tests. Ask several others who have just taken the tests about the conditions of the testing sites. I have even had a couple of friends sign up at the last minute, and because of being so late, they were assigned to a university in another town. Not only did they have to get up extra early to travel, but they also had to find the

room they were testing in on a large college campus. Talk about added stress. If that were the case and you had no other choice but to take it in a strange and unknown land, it might be a good idea to go a day or so ahead of time to find the testing site.

There are also sites where you can sign up for classes to help improve your scores, but many times there is a cost to go along with it. Just make sure it is a reputable site (such as Kaplan or Sylvan) with facts of improved scores. And as with everything else, ask others if they have taken these courses or know someone who has.

Lastly, be prepared. Make sure, as simple as it seems, to remember to take the correct type of calculator (which is stated when you are signing up) as well as your ID. Forgetting your calculator can really mess up your math scores, and not having an ID could prevent you from taking the test.

Before continuing, I would like to share with you the fact that, while I was researching this book and trying to amass case studies, almost nobody recalled anything at all about the tests whether they had just taken them a couple of years ago or even just the previous year. One young woman, whose story is not included in this book, told me she recalled more about taking her General Education Diploma (GED) than the SAT — and she is now a college graduate with a full-time career. She swears she has no recollection of her scores, but obviously, they were high enough to grant her acceptance in the college of her choice.

I finally found one student, whose story is related toward the end of this chapter, but the point I am trying to make here is that — like so many other things in life — what may seem to be an insurmountable challenge (or a monster under the bed, as I will discuss later) is normally forgotten as soon as it has been finished (or slain). All that worry, all that fuss, and — *Wow, I do not even recall it.*

All right; let's continue. Despite the scores that you might achieve on standardized tests, there are many issues going on behind the scenes that extend beyond individual numeric scores. For example, colleges and universities seeking to admit certain types of applicants are more likely to consider those individuals who obtain the highest scores within the selected applicant pool. The unfortunate reality is that you might perform to the best of your ability during a standardized testing situation, obtain an acceptable score, and yet fail to impress the admissions committee, especially if they have observed higher scores from other applicants who might (for whatever reason) be more impressive overall. Do not get discouraged by this bit of news; you will get there and accomplish your objectives regardless. Sometimes you have to take those stepping stones to get there (as previously stated), such as going to a community college for the first portion of your education. Most times it is easier to get into a four-year college or university when you transfer with your associate degree in hand. The test scores have little influence in their acceptance at this level. Another benefit of going to

a community college, as mentioned before, is the cost savings and the difficulty level of the classes. You just need to remain calm and optimistic throughout the application process and remember that standardized tests are only a part of the total application process, and that many other criteria are considered.

The standardized test serves a multi-dimensional purpose in the college admissions process. Primarily, it determines if you fit the minimum academic criteria for admission, based upon the score(s) that you achieved. Furthermore, this test score also enables an admissions committee to determine how you might fare in their academic programs over the course of your college career. You might discover that this test serves as a deal-breaker in many college admission situations, and that if you do not fare well on the test with respect to admission standards, you are not likely to gain admission without significant effort in other areas, such as were discussed in the previous chapter.

So far as the tests go, though, your best opportunity to determine if you will gain measurable success in the standardized admissions process for college is through taking the PSAT early in the junior year of high school. This test, also known as the Preliminary SAT, is divided into three distinct sections (math, reading, and writing), and in some schools, this test is required. Ironically enough, one of my non-case study people recalled well the PSAT and not one thing about the SAT — once again, how strange this seems. Anyway, the most feasible strategy that comes highly recommended by many professionals is to take the PSAT test as early as possible in the high school year, as it shows a candid ability to predict how you might perform on the SAT and will enable you to prepare more effectively for the real thing. You should pay attention in your sophomore year to determine if your school offers the PSAT and if you are eligible to sign up. It is in your best interest to pursue this opportunity to ensure that you have as many chances as possible to develop an affinity for the standardized testing experience early on in high school. The PSAT is used as a tool to determine those who are National Merit Scholars. For this, you need to score in the top 90 percent nationwide, but only test scores during your junior year counts towards this. And do not worry; you do not have to be one of the few in the top 90 percent to gain admissions to the college of your choice.

Standardized tests commonly serve as a gauge regarding how a student will perform in a pressure-filled situation that is limited by time constraints.

This type of scenario is desirable to college admissions experts for a number of reasons, most notably that this situation is likely to assimilate many real-life college testing situations, where significant amounts of material must be memorized or recalled in a short period of time. This is particularly important in science- and mathematics-based coursework, although other subjects also require you to recall information in a similar capacity. As a result, the way in which you perform on the SAT or ACT will serve as a universal guide regarding your ability to convey information in a comparable testing environment. Because testing is an important part of any college setting, admissions committees want to recognize that applicants are adequately prepared to manage these situations successfully whenever required.

But, on an overall global scale, just how important are your test scores? In *The New Rules of College Admissions*, Kramer and London are quite adamant in that colleges look to hold their own academic ranking by admitting only those students who will perform well grade-wise. The standardized tests offer a good indication of those who will help keep — or improve — the rankings, and those are the only students who will be accepted.

Yet, the issue is not always quite so bluntly stated, and over the years, there has been much debate and re-analysis of the importance of these examinations; high school transcripts can be held equally if not more highly indicative of a student's potential. A good example of the ongoing debate over transcript-against-standardized tests can be found in Michele A. Hernández's *A Is For Admission*. As evidenced in her work, the former Dartmouth College Assistant Director of Admissions has had to re-examine the issue and has changed her opinion over time. Whereas she once felt it was unfair to base a student's future entirely upon a single afternoon's work (compared with the years of education leading up to that afternoon), high school rankings are not always accurately indicative of a student's adaptability to the college realm.

According to Hernández, some high schools are loath to even use rankings because it may encourage unhealthy competition and foster bad feelings among students. But even when students are ranked, high school class rankings do not give equal weight when making overall comparisons based on transcripts alone. For example, a student who placed first in his graduating class of 50 will rank higher (numerically speaking) than one who placed 42nd in a class of over 600. Nevertheless, one must consider the difficulty of curriculum and also the overall capability of the class. Perhaps that number-one student attended a rural, under-funded high school in the South, whose overall curriculum will undoubtedly "lose" when compared with a state-of-the-art, wealthy parochial high school in New York. Still, this young man did graduate No. 1, and he and four other students will rightfully be able to "pad" their college applications with the fact they placed in the top 10 percent of their class.

Regardless of all the debate, standardized tests are here to stay, and you might as well face the fact you will be taking at least one of them — even if you will never recall anything about it. But there is another helpful thing to remember. Almost every college will "superscore" your test results. Superscore means they are taking the best score from each section of multiple tests and using the best score for that section to average your overall score. For example, if you were to take the SAT three times, they would use the highest math score from these tests and average it with the highest verbal score from any of these three tests, which can result in an overall higher score. However, some colleges will only superscore SAT and not ACT, while others will superscore either one.

All right, so let's say you took the test, and bombed. Big time. Although a heavily-weighted and less-than-expected standardized test score might seem unfair (you had a real bad sinus headache that day or the car broke down on the way and you barely got there in time), the fact remains that some schools will give more credence to the score than others. The SAT and ACT tests may also demonstrate strengths or weaknesses in given subject areas, such as mathematics and reading comprehension, and it is likely that these differences are also reflected in other measurable forms of academic performance that extend beyond these tests, such as your grades or the difficulty level of the classes you have taken. Nonetheless, it does not seem right to judge a student's ability by that one day's examination, and the perceived "strengths and weaknesses" (particularly the latter) on that given day may be misleading in the overall scheme of things so far as you are concerned. And yet, this by and large can be the case, so you must be prepared for the possibility.

This is one of the unexpected obstacles of which I spoke earlier; how you respond to it and make adjustments accordingly will perhaps be the most telling of all regarding your ability to succeed in college. Regardless of your prior academic achievement, your inability to concentrate through the pounding sinus pressure on one rainy Saturday afternoon or worrying about how much it will take to fix your car may limit or exclude you from some colleges or universities as a result of your scores — okay, fine. There are other schools, and you will have ample opportunity to perform better on future tests. Keep your options open (I will talk later about choosing several schools) and you will eventually find the best overall fit.

But wait — all we have discussed so far is the possibility of a poor test results. Although standardized testing may be difficult for some, it is amazingly simple for others, and more often than not, these are the students who also excel academically in most subject areas. Of course, what standardized paper or digital tests cannot reveal are the other aspects of a developing college-bound student (recall the aloof genius of whom I spoke of earlier and this is where good high school transcripts can possibly balance out the test scores). Unlike mere report cards, transcripts reveal a more well-rounded review of the student's high school experience; the progression of classes and grades reflected there will be far more informative than any given day's one-time test results. Let's also not forget that how you perform once you are in college will be a further reflection of your overall character and chances for success; if you apply yourself, those test scores and other academic standards will almost certainly rise further than you might have imagined — even if you are not "genius" material. Here is a terrific case study example from the one student I found who actually recalled his test:

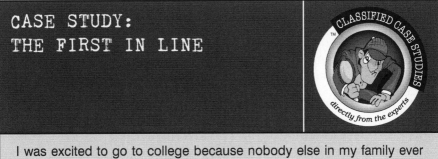

CASE STUDY:
THE FIRST IN LINE

CLASSIFIED CASE STUDIES
TM
directly from the experts

I was excited to go to college because nobody else in my family ever had. I had also seen co-workers at the dead-end jobs who were not going anywhere and probably never would. When I first decided to go to college, I initially was going to enroll in a community college and just be satisfied with a two-year associate degree. It was shortly after

I graduated from high school that I decided to go to a university and get a four-year bachelor's degree with the intention of continuing on to graduate school.

I knew I wanted to stay close to home, so I began to look at local schools. My first choice was the University of Cincinnati. After contemplating exactly what I wanted to major in, I decided to apply at Northern Kentucky University. Within a few short days of applying, I received a letter in the mail congratulating my acceptance and also a congratulatory phone call from the university. I was now enrolled as a full-time student majoring in computer science.

Before applying to any university, I had to take one of many exams in order to get accepted. I choose to take the ACT while still in my senior year in high school. Preparing for the ACT was a simple process, due to the amount of available material and prep courses. However, after the test was taken and the results were in, I was by no means pleased with the score that I got. I decided to retake the exam, this time getting much higher than the first but not exactly what I wanted. Although my score was high enough to get into NKU, I personally was not pleased. But I decided to let it go and not really bother me because although my score was not the top, I knew I would be OK.

I just finished my second year at NKU, and am currently on the Dean's List, aided by a 4.0 GPA in my third semester. Since the beginning, I have changed majors twice and finally decided to finish out my bachelor's degree double-majoring in construction management and construction technology. Deciding to go to a university was the best decision that I have ever made. Although my ACT score was not what I wanted it to be, the two years that I have been at NKU have proven to me that I can do anything that I want to do — all I have to do is set my mind to it.

—Justin Thompson, Student, Northern Kentucky University

As Mr. Thompson's story shows, standardized test results are not the end-all; you do not have to "kiss your college dreams good-bye" if you don't get the score you want. Nonetheless, when taking standardized tests, as always, you must perform to the utmost of your ability to develop the best opportunities for success. These test score(s) are taken into consideration at least to some degree for virtually every college or university, some much more than others, and you must make all possible efforts to perform at a satisfactory, and preferably better, level.

Mr. Thompson also stated he did much better the second time he took the ACT. This is true in taking almost any type of test; knowing what is expected from you, and the type of test that you are taking, is always a huge help in any testing situation.

Grit your teeth through that headache, take non-drowsy sinus relief medication, forget about the car for these next few hours, and give this test all you have because it <u>will</u> matter. This may be an unfortunate circumstance, but it clearly demonstrates that overall academic performance — in transcripts and testing — is critical, along with all the other things we are discussing in developing a successful portfolio for college admissions.

COLLEGE APPLICATION

Chapter 5

Did Someone Say *Options?*

Let's review what we have discussed thus far. You have self-reflected, sat down and had some of those serious post-high school dialoguing with parents, teachers, and counselors, and have decided that you are indeed college-bound. You have started thinking about what kind of college might interest you and listed your most basic priorities. You have taken the standardized tests, and — most important of all — you have truly "buckled down" to make the most of your remaining high school days, both with your curriculum and grades, as well as your extracurricular and community service activities.

At the advice of your guidance counselor, you have gotten a clearer idea of just when and how to begin the application process. In addition, you have begun some online research and sent off for information from various institutions that caught your interest, and the mailbox is overstuffed — perhaps even with some basic information from schools (postcards, single-page flyers) you did not actively request but that somehow found out you are college-shopping. (Ah, the wonders of modern technology!) My personal response regarding such unsolicited materials would most likely be to pitch 'em — but then again, throughout my life, I have been roundly scolded for my aversion to "clutter," and just maybe I have shortchanged myself a time or two. Perhaps the better way to deal with these materials would be to set them aside in their own pile and concentrate on those you requested; the unsolicited ones can always be investigated later if you somehow have the need or energy to do so. But if your mailbox has remained empty, do not despair; more and more colleges send emails and online information.

Be prepared; if you are serious about making the right college selection, you will find yourself wading through veritable oceans of brochures, pamphlets, course handbooks, and the not so proverbial searches on their websites you attempt to identify the colleges that are most appealing to you.

During this period, you will no doubt find the options overwhelming, with considerable choices in colleges and universities throughout the country. Private against public, liberal arts against specialty, pre-med or pre-law against mathematics, large against small; the list goes on. Each of these options requires you to examine a variety of criteria, and it is important to develop the previously begun list to enhance and narrow your college-application choices. Optimistically, the range of colleges to which you have sent indications of interest have already been gleaned from that first list of priorities discussed in Chapter 2. For example, if you want to be near a beach and consider this to be extremely vital, you in all probability should not plan to apply to the University of Nebraska, and if the beach is the most important aspect of your choice of colleges, then perhaps you need to reevaluate the *why* of going to college.

But now what? How do you begin to narrow the field? Although we have been laying the foundations all along, this chapter will further address the many options that you have when considering all aspects of college, and these will help you determine the best course of action that satisfies your personal strengths and needs as you construct your application plans.

As mentioned previously, the first step in this process is to develop a selection strategy that will eliminate colleges and universities that do not align with your own criteria or key strengths. Let's forget about the desired beach locale for now, because even though that is exceedingly important to you, there are more practical issues to consider. For example, if your high school GPA is 3.2, it would almost certainly not be wise to consider an Ivy League school such as Harvard or Yale, because your chances of admission are almost nonexistent. This is not meant to be discouraging; rather, it is a realistic way to begin narrowing your options. It is unwise to waste precious time reading about a college or university that does not fit your knowledge and skill set. You can easily go to the college's website to find out their requirements for acceptance. Most of them will tell you the average range of GPA and test scores that were accepted the previous year, and a few may just state whether admissions is difficult, average, or easy. Also, let's not forget that Ivy League schools tend to come with an incredibly large price tag attached, and unfortunately, the reality of where you are going to attend will usually depend on the cost. Those with financial need, as defined by FAFSA, tend to fare better — because if they are accepted to an Ivy League college, the school will find ways to fund their education. However, this knocks out lower middle class to upper middle class students when it comes to attending, as their families cannot afford to pay the high costs of some of these colleges.

Since money is a concern for most of us, I would also recommend that when you further develop your selection criteria, you consider the financial aspects related to state-funded opposed to private colleges and universities. If you decide on a public university located within your home state, the tuition rate is likely to be much lower than at an out-of-state institution for which you would be charged a higher out-of-state tuition rate (sometimes the cost of out-of-state can actually be tripled for non-residents). There are also some colleges that may waive the out-of-state fee or even have a scholarship for that purpose. And if that particular college is one that you absolutely have to attend (perhaps one of the few with your major), find out if they will allow you to be counted as a resident after one year of attending their school, as many of them will. Just remember, if you have to pay the full cost for a non-resident of that particular state, and you are striving for a four-year or more degree, you most likely will be much better off financially attending a less expensive college for the first two years. You can then get your associate degree at a much lower cost and then transfer to that more expensive out-of-state college. You can actually save quite a bit of money for those two short years at a local college. Beware also of non-accredited private schools. They offer essay acceptance, small classes, and many promises. Before moving on, I should mention that if you happen to live in an area near a state border, there may be a "reciprocity" agreement; for instance, my hometown of Cincinnati, Ohio is located at a precise junction of three states: Ohio, Kentucky, and Indiana. Northern Kentucky University, located just south of Cincinnati in Fort Thomas, offers the following in its online catalog at **www.nku.edu**:

> "A metropolitan university, Northern takes advantage of its close proximity to other higher education and post-secondary institutions through reciprocity agreements with the University of Cincinnati, Cincinnati State Technical and Community College, and Southern State Community College. Northern serves Indiana students through a reciprocity agreement with the State of Indiana. The University also provides applied research, service, and continuing education programs related to the needs of its region."

Reciprocity can refer to either transferring of grades, financial costs, or both. As indicated in the above paragraph, there is a mutual agreement among these colleges to accept each other's students with no additional "out-of-state" charges added to tuition costs.

At any rate, state schools are consistently lower-priced than private schools, and therefore your selection criteria might reflect these exclusions. Your best option is to examine the costs associated with a full-time course load, in addition to books and other fees, and to determine if you will live on campus or if you live close enough to commute from home to class. (Of course, at today's gas prices, either choice could save you quite a bit of money over the long term, depending on the proximity of your home to school.) Although it is perfectly natural at this stage of life to want and feel the need to maintain some degree of independence by living the dorm or off-campus apartment life, you must be realistic about the additional financial burdens this may bring. What do the dorms cost, and what-all is included in those fees (food and parking)? How reasonable, clean, and safe are the apartments? Believe it or not, cost of living is normally (unless you attend a private school) much more than the tuition and fees. Again, for most students, the financial considerations of college selection are perhaps the most critical; therefore, this information must be obtained as early as possible in the research and planning process so that your options are fully explored and all possible limitations are identified — and excluded — up front.

A note: in an earlier chapter, I touched on scholarship opportunities, but at this stage, let's not factor them in. Unless you are the star quarterback or outstanding Rhodes Scholar material, scholarships are not guaranteed and therefore should not be included in your search at present. Also, many seniors receive scholarships for their freshman year, but most of those scholarships are not renewable. So, although you may have the first year paid for with those scholarships, the money stops after that, and you need to make sure that you have a way to pay for the following years as well. After you have narrowed your choices, you may then wish to explore the possibilities along those channels.

Once the financing concern has been addressed, you should also explore other issues related to selecting the most appropriate college or university that will best suit your needs. There are a number of factors that should be considered, including curricular offerings, class size, and overall academic strengths within your selected major — or the best programs for undecided-at-present majors. Also, what extracurricular and other outside activities are being offered? Another focus to think of is the internships and job placement opportunities available for you. Many times the type of career that you may choose, and the place that will hire you, can depend on the internships you do during the summers, and many colleges have better internship and placement records than others. Weighing and comparing all these factors may seem particularly daunting at first; but once you have pared the number of colleges down to a select few, the evaluations will become easier. A careful and thorough approach to your analyses will establish the tone for the entire college application and admission process (not to mention your upcoming class work), so it is wise to get into these good habits early on in the game.

I cannot help it; at this point, I truly need to deliver a stern lecture. The polar opposite of a "good habit" is that most frustrating p-word: *procrastination*, which for some reason tends to hit many seniors harder than most (a reoccurring symptom of the dreaded "senioritis" disease). As a student, I dared not attempt it as did many of my peers, and as a composition instructor, I positively raged (internally, of course; I deliberately kept my facial expression and body language neutral) when my students received p-word-related failing grades. They had plenty of time and knew well in advance, both from their syllabus and my oft-repeated reminders, what was expected, and when it was due — and bear in mind, this was college, so they should have learned from earlier mistakes by now. Procrastination is habitual, and some people <u>swear</u> they do better (they work "faster," yes, but not "better") when feeling time-pressure, but I cannot express just how badly this can hurt you in your college search.

Wait a minute — I hear some dissent. Yes, it is true that educational institutions themselves often seem to procrastinate when it comes to selecting which students will be accepted. A June 2008 article in *USA Today* stated the fact that many high school graduates still do not know where they will be attending college in the fall, and this is still true today. These are students whose applications were timely and complete, and they are still having to play the waiting ... waiting ... waiting game. Although I certainly do not pretend to understand the process, nor do I defend or denounce whatever procedures colleges and universities take, the bottom line is that at least these students who are waiting did their part so far as being timely. In spite of the momentarily uncertainty, they are already well on the way. They cannot be responsible for a college's procrastination. But they themselves did what they had to do — in the time allotted — or they would not even be on that grueling waiting-to-hear list.

I repeat: although the actual selection process might take some time, and even after you have applied, the wait might be long, the worst mistake you can make is to put off beginning the investigation and exploration phase. The decisions you are facing will affect the rest of your life and therefore must be addressed accordingly: timely and with concerted attention. Making a wise ultimate choice requires the ability to analyze, evaluate, and absorb a large amount of information over time; therefore, the sooner you begin, the better. Do not expect to "wing it" at the last minute or read over ten applications and their diverse directions in one afternoon. Start the process as soon as possible and allow yourself time to fully explore all the materials made available to you. As applications are basically all done online, you need to remember that each college website is different, and finding out all of the information that you need to research can take time to find it for each college that you are investigating.

One last thought on my p-word diatribe: take note, you are not the only student who is college-bound. You are not the only one to whom the colleges have sent letters or emails to encourage you to attend, and there are many more who would be willing to take your place — and some of them (believe it or not) will not be procrastinators. They are the ones who are no longer holding their breaths, as they already know that they will indeed be going somewhere in the fall. If you truly want to go to college, and have an opportunity to apply for/be admitted to the school that will best suit you, do not waste any time. A late application could definitely result in not be accepted, and if it is a rolling admissions (one that accepts students pretty much year round), you could still be too late to get any of the automatic incoming freshman scholarships (as they are usually given out early in the year) or it could also result in you being put on a wait list if they are already full.

I have spoken; no more p-word lectures — at least in this chapter. (Any of my former students would tell you that you have gotten off pretty darn easily.)

Okay, back to the chapter's subject: sorting the options. For some students, the college application experience is relatively simple; they may have only two schools in mind when they begin the process, with one far and above the other, and upon gaining acceptance to both, the choice is made almost immediately. Nonetheless, for most students, this process is not frequently so cut-and-dried; a variety of colleges seem appealing, and therefore it is often extremely difficult to make the decisions entirely on their own.

So, you are not one of the lucky ones with only two options. How many of the x-amount colleges whose brochures or websites that you have researched, studied, and found appealing should you seriously apply to? According to *The New Rules of College Admission*, the ideal number should be seven. Authors Kramer and London break down this figure into a 2:3:2 ratio, with the first two being ideal, the middle three being just right, and the last two being adequate for your needs. You may consider this to number be too confining, or conversely, too many, but what the authors are trying to do is help you narrow your choices while still giving some latitude. The challenge of comparing schools is more easily dealt with by realizing that of the colleges you may have inquired about, there does come a point in which the field must be pared down into a reasonable size.

If you are of an athletic mind (and if you are not, bear with me), picture the "March Madness" of NCAA basketball. Over 60 teams start off in the tournament (with half of them eliminated immediately), and the brackets gradually work their way down to Sweet 16, Elite Eight, Final Four, and then the championship game. Now, no one expects you to have investigated 60 schools (if you did, wow, that is just fine), but the truth is that like any truly "weak" team that somehow found its way into the tourney, many of the colleges that originally appealed to you will immediately be discarded for one reason or another. In keeping as closely as possible to with Kramer and London in this analogy, "Elite Eight" is closest to what you should consider for application, and if all eight colleges offer you acceptance, you may have to go through your own version of the Final Four before deciding the champion. Another huge help in making your final choices, as I have already said more than once, would be to actually physically visit the colleges. Believe it or not, each college has a completely different atmosphere to it. The pictures on the website may look great, but it is still another story when you go there to see it for yourself in person. I have friends who were die-hard fans of a particular college, and they when they went on a tour of the "opposing" school, they changed their minds by the way they were treated and the way the campus, the students, and the atmosphere made them feel. Many times, if you know your major and, if you are lucky, visiting that particular department and speaking to a professor or student in that department can be a life-changing experience as well.

At some point along the way, but especially at the Elite Eight, you may want to investigate any school-sponsored scholarship possibilities. A scholarship will unquestionably influence your decision, but recall that all things should be considered, and this process, with or without possible scholarship assistance, can be quite intimidating and exhausting. In some ways, it was easier when the field was larger (again, picture March Madness; at the onset of the tournament, any one of 60-plus teams is still in the picture), but now that the scope has tightened, more exacting criteria must be considered. Scholarships are only one of the many factors still demanding examination, and by now, you have most likely been thinking so much and so hard about all this that your head feels worse than it did the rain-drenched day you plodded through the SAT. As referred to before, many colleges have automatic freshmen scholarships that depend solely on your GPA and test scores, and many times, the higher the SAT/ACT scores, the higher the scholarship dollars. Some of the Ivy League schools even offer financial aid if you are in need in grants and scholarships and not in loans. You may also get accepted into one school's honors program and not the others. There are usually many perks to honors in college, such as smaller classes, first choice of courses, and sometimes even scholarships. As each school differs in what they offer financially, this is something else that you need to research and take into consideration as well.

Do not worry; you are well on your way, and you are in reality not as "alone" as it may seem. I highly urge and recommend that you talk over your frustrations and concerns with your parents, guidance counselors, teachers, and friends so that you will be better able to narrow down which college or colleges will be appropriate for you. Although (as has been stated repeatedly) you alone can make the final decision, simply talking things over with someone else — having a fresh "ear" to listen to your concerns — may ease the confusion. It goes without saying that when the only voice you are hearing is your own, you are limited as to what your answers may be; someone else might be able to offer a whole new perspective or solution that clarifies things. There is an old adage about not being able to see the forest for the trees — well, a fresh opinion or suggestion just may chop down a few trees and make that forest seem less formidable.

There is no reason to feel ashamed or that you appear incapable; chances are that you could clear a few trees in someone else's forest of confusion. Recall my story about Mrs. G's English class? She had been reading "Richard Cory" for — literally — well over 30 years, and had never been able to clear the meaning of a certain line, but an introverted 14-year-old ninth-grader did just that. The point is that open discussion and a different perspective(s) can help you solve or eliminate at least one problematic issue, and thus be able to move ahead in your quest for a final decision. But I may have gotten ahead of myself a bit; here I have you selecting from the Elite Eight who want to include you in their student body, and we have not even discussed the application process itself. I will close this chapter with an appropriate case study that addresses narrowing college choices and also the main reason for this book: writing the applications essay.

CASE STUDY: AT THE CROSSROADS

I applied to several universities while I was a senior at an all girls' college prep academy in Cincinnati, Ohio. I decided to only apply to five colleges due to the fact that I did not want to go too far from home, but I also did not want to stay in-state. I, with my senioritis setting in, also did not want to have to take the SAT II, which some universities required for their application. Therefore, I applied to Purdue, Indiana University, Marquette University, Emory University, and Washington University in St. Louis, and I did get into all five schools. I finally decided to attend Washington University due to their excellent pre-medical biology program, overall reputation, and gorgeous campus. I also decided to run on their varsity track and field team.

As I recall, the most difficult part of the application was writing the essay! The essay usually asks you to talk about some aspect of your personality or your career goals. As an 18-year-old, I was not exactly sure what I wanted to do with my life. I began thinking about what had impacted me the most in my life so far, and what things I truly enjoyed doing.

Overall, I think that the most challenging part of writing any essay is the introduction. I have a difficult time writing an introduction sentence that captures the audience but also conveys what the subject of my paper will be. I usually start by making a list of ideas, terms, and phrases that come to mind when I think about the subject of my essay. This gets my thought process going and prevents me from leaving anything out of the essay. I start by writing a little about each idea that I came up with, and eventually I connect those ideas to each other in order to make the essay flow.

Although I do not write often, I find writing to be cathartic. Whether it is writing an email to a friend or journaling about an event in my life, I find that writing enables me to get my feelings out on paper and think more clearly. I think that being able to write and express oneself is very important especially when it comes to applying for jobs, graduate school, or even just to communicate with others. I feel that writing skills are a reflection of one's personality, style, creativity, personal experiences, and education.

—Valerie Lasko, Research Assistant
University of Cincinnati College of Medicine

By the way, as I will discuss further a bit later on, Valerie was able to use the same essay for all five applications, thus easing the stress of having to come up with a different essay for each of her chosen colleges. However, this is usually only normal when you are using the common application to apply to more than one college. Most state colleges have their own separate essay, so be prepared to write more than just one. And while some colleges may give you different essay prompts, they are often looking for the same information — which allows you to tweak and draw from one essay to make things a little easier.

One more thing to think about: not all colleges require an essay for their applications. For example most community colleges, and even some four-year colleges, have short and brief applications, without an essay question, as well as no questions pertaining to your extracurricular or community services. Some just need to know if you have graduated with the correct courses and college entrance exams to attend, or they may just base their decision solely on your GPA and SAT and/or ACT scores. The essay can also be optional, but optional usually means "do it" in many cases.

In conclusion to this chapter, here is a case study from Valerie's brother, whose college application and acceptance were far less stressful; he had only one choice that appealed to him, and there was no written application.

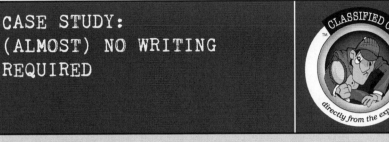

CASE STUDY: (ALMOST) NO WRITING REQUIRED

I sent written application to only one college, DeVry University. DeVry was founded in Chicago, Illinois. There are now campuses all over the United States from coast-to-coast. DeVry is a four-year institution that awards associate and bachelor's degrees. They now have master's level programs in business and technology. They also offer medical technology degrees.

The application was easy. The recruiter came to my school and then met with me and my parents at our house, and I was accepted to DeVry in Columbus, Ohio almost right away. I received a Bachelor of Science degree in 2007 majoring in computer engineering technology.

There was never any question that my skills laid in the area of mathematics and computers. I attended a vocational and technical high school in Cincinnati, Ohio. Writing was never my forte. I knew early on in my education that I was writing-challenged when it came to book reports and essays. Even the shortest assignments seemed too long.

Many teachers and instructors tried to encourage me, but none succeeded. I just did not like to write. I found that "hands-on" activities and assignments were more rewarding. I have mechanical skills and enjoy building engines and working on cars. Computers always fascinated me, so I chose a college that would enhance and develop my technical abilities.

I have to admit that writing skills are more important than I thought now that I am employed as a systems analyst for a large corporation. I write official emails on a daily basis, so I have to be able to express myself well. But at least they're not as long as those school assignments.

—Richard S. Lasko, Systems Analyst

Chapter 6

Selecting Students: A College's "Write"

Thus far, with a limited remark or two in Chapter 4, we have discussed the college admissions process from the prospective student's point of view. In some ways, the process of selecting future students has remained fairly standard over the course of time, but — especially within the past 50 years or so — there have been many new developments that paradoxically help and hinder the overall academic performance and expectations of students and educational institutions to which they apply. The most obvious of such a simultaneous paradox is the advent of computer technology, which has resulted in a better way of managing databases such as student transcripts and standardized testing, but which has also encouraged a certain degree of laziness in the modern student, particularly as it applies to writing.

The following case study, written by a 55-year-old mother of four who possesses a master's degree in social work, is a wonderful all-around illustration of the changes she has observed during her lifetime as far as college-bound student education is concerned, and also is a good introduction to this chapter.

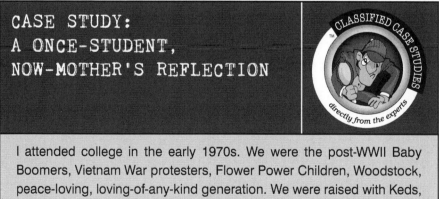

CASE STUDY:
A ONCE-STUDENT,
NOW-MOTHER'S REFLECTION

CLASSIFIED CASE STUDIES
directly from the experts

I attended college in the early 1970s. We were the post-WWII Baby Boomers, Vietnam War protesters, Flower Power Children, Woodstock, peace-loving, loving-of-any-kind generation. We were raised with Keds, hoola-hoops, Dr. Spock, nuclear families, and stay-at-home moms.

I recall one of my own experiences in high school that encouraged my interest in academics. My 7th grade teacher had just purchased the *Great Books of the Western World* collection. He had the opportunity to select one student from his classes to read specific passages and answer questions. If one completed the task, he or she could potentially earn a college scholarship. I was very honored to be the student chosen, not only for the challenge, but because I was also allowed to take the books home.

Our generation assumed that we would go straight to college after high school. Taking a job in the "real world" to get "life experience" was not an option for most of us. And we were prepared. Our primary and secondary education focused on the three Rs; reading, writing and 'rithmetic. We mastered writing; our grammar and vocabulary skills were impeccable. Furthermore, WE did the work, not technology. We read from real books and encyclopedias and researched in libraries with walls. Most papers were handwritten unless we were fortunate enough to own a typewriter, preferably an "iconic" Smith-Corona (name-brand business machine, not the beer, as my children's generation know it).

After college and having pursued a continuing academic career for a brief time, I took on the challenge of raising four children of my own. As a parent, my goal was to guide each of these very different individuals down a path that would develop their unique skills and talents. The end result is: a biology major and researcher and graduate of a private mid-western university; a photographer, artist, and Communications Master's Degree graduate from a prestigious European university; a systems analyst from a highly recognized technical university, and a social work/psychology major pending graduation from a state university close to home.

Although I am proud to say that each of my children is succeeding, one thing I've really been able to see through their college experiences is: this generation hasn't learned to write. The basics of grammar, penmanship, composition, and spelling have not been mastered as modern day computers supersede traditional educational methods. Our schools today opt for group projects, hands-on learning versus lengthy book reports and essays.

Children today are involved in extensive extracurricular activities, far more than we grew up with. With the impact of the two-parent working household and women in careers outside the home, evenings and weekends are busy playing "catch-up" on household tasks and driving kids long distances to a variety of outside activities. School assignments that involve reading books and writing with parental support are often not a priority. I believe it is the parents' responsibility and also the teachers' to impress upon students the impact of writing skills throughout life in work-related and personal activities and also in their academic pursuits.

Unfortunately, colleges today are having to do remedial work with students entering their academic programs. In one of my daughter's college orientation programs, the parents and students were told there would be extensive writing expected throughout their college classes. Because of this expectation, many of these students with delayed reading and writing skills must participate in the writing labs and remedial tutoring programs. For some, they are learning to enjoy and value writing for the first time in their lives. I have observed one of my daughters, in the social work program at Wright State University, developing self-confidence in relation to her mastery of writing.

—Joan Lasko, M.S.W.

Along this vein, one of the professors for whom I grad-assisted (but who prefers to remain anonymous) used to remind her students of a statistic she once heard that suggested over $70 billion is being lost by American hospitals and businesses every year because middle-management people cannot write clearly (so maybe that is one of the reasons why health insurance rates are so high). Anyway, here is another opinion, spoken from a professional educator's point of view, which echoes the comments above:

CASE STUDY:
"SHOW 'EM THE DOOR
(NICELY)"

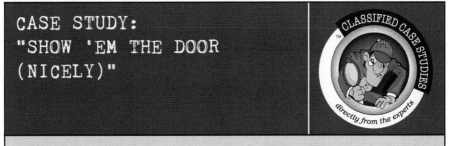

I attended the University of Cincinnati, Union Institute and University, and Antioch-Yellow Springs, Ohio, which I selected because I had an Ohio Board of Regents Scholarship that required that I attend grad school in Ohio. Also, Antioch was the only school that offered the psychology program I needed.

During my ongoing pursuits of post-graduate psychology studies, I have facilitated addiction support groups and counseled many fragile human beings whose lives just need some positive influence. I have also held various legal secretary positions in some of my city's largest and most prestigious law firms. They demand excellence, as do I, from anything I type, transcribe or write for them. I am not much of a creative writer (well, maybe a few wine-fortified free-verse poetry attempts over the years), but I am gratified when something I write results in somebody learning or gaining needed information.

It is easy to understand how some students might become resistant to writing. It is not always easy, and sometimes outside forces make it seem even worse. Back in college, I had an instructor, who, for simplicity's sake, I shall call "Smith." He was a total JERK! He did not teach English; he belittled students. After he ridiculed one of my papers, I stood up in class and told him that he was not teaching English but was teaching a course in "Smith." Needless to say, I flunked the course. At that point in my life, he turned me off to academic pursuits but not to writing — which he could easily have done with his arrogance.

Fortunately, at Union Institute, when I returned to college in 1998, there was a marvelous instructor who taught the survey course in Composition/Literature. When I got an "A" on my very first paper, along with words of praise for a job well-done, I felt validated and redeemed. Smith had been conquered!

However, it must also be said that writing is very important, and I am disturbed at the levels to which it seems to be taught in high schools today. Although I could never have been as rude or discouraging as Smith, when I taught (Legal Assistant/Legal Secretary/Paralegal classes in a community college), at the first class session I required my students to demonstrate their command of English by writing a simple paragraph. If they failed in this assignment, I would suggest (as kindly and constructively as possible) that they pursue a different course of study, because my program required students with high "verbal" skills.

This introductory exercise was where I saw how badly things have really become. I've been watching the steady decline in writing skills for the past five decades. What I learned in high school in the '50s is now considered college-level writing, and — more often than not — I was dismayed to see the results of the paragraph assignment.

—Eileen Andrews, Legal Assistant/College Instructor

So, even if it is true (as Ms. Andrews suggests) that college-level writing has slowly but gradually sunk to lower standards, and even if remedial courses are often necessary (as Ms. Lasko can avouch), the fact remains that there are standards, and if you meet or exceed them, the better your chances of admission. And if remedial courses are really needed, perhaps that stepping stone of a community college might be the best route for that student.

As has always been the case, today's colleges and universities seek to admit students that fit their desired mold, which will be formed by a variety of different criteria according to the individual school. As a prospective student, your responsibility is to identify these selection requirements and to determine if you might fit effectively into the chosen model. We have for the most part covered the basics of all that in the previous chapters; now, you must also consider the fact that colleges seek to admit only the most qualified applicants for their programs, and — current writing levels notwithstanding — that they have gained a larger degree of selectivity in admissions in recent years, and this only seems to be more demanding as time goes on.

Many prestigious colleges have always maintained their reputations by recruiting only those students who satisfy a firmly established, high-caliber set of criteria. This is particularly true for Ivy League colleges and universities, and also many private schools. Yet, public colleges and universities have also increased their requirements for selectivity to admit only those students who are most likely to succeed, as this is a reflection of the colleges' success as academic institutions. With the number of higher-education institutions growing every year, there is increased competition among them for strong student candidates (a.k.a. good, well-rounded potential alumni [but not "rounded" as in Uncle Joe]) to help a college or university stay "on top of the academia game."

Bear in mind that colleges and universities are businesses. And like any manufacturer or producer, they must use only the best ingredients or materials to make a good, marketable final product that encourages more people to buy in the future. After all, as with any enterprise, they are in business to produce good results, which will increase their chances of being able to stay in business for years to come despite the ever-increasing competition from other such entities. Therefore, realistically, it is just not logical for a college to admit a student with a poor GPA, low test scores, and a flimsy record of accomplishment — or one who shows a definite weakness in — or, perhaps more than a definite weakness, an *obvious aversion* to written expression.

Wait — that is still not a good way to phrase it; let's try this: an obvious aversion to <u>wanting to improve</u> written expression. A limitation in the area of writing can be addressed; are you not applying to college to learn and improve yourself? The aversion to writing may always exist, but as you have no doubt heard *ad infinitum, ad nauseam* from your parents and teachers, there will always be things you have to do that you would prefer not to.

If you have not learned that unhappy lesson by now, this will no doubt become a major part of your continuing education.

At any rate, even as you invest in applying to a college, that college or university must also weigh the advantages of investing in its applicants. Good writing skills, and even more so the willingness to build upon them, are a strong indicator to the college that you are indeed an "ingredient" who may benefit their final product — which, after all, includes you. Believe it or not, even more than the school-logo sweatshirt or ball cap you wear, your writing skills in the real world just may be the best advertisement for the institution ... and they will certainly be one of your best selling points (along with your college degree) when you go to offer yourself to a future employer.

Before I continue, and because I can sense the dismay and objections already coming my way (which I will address in another chapter), let me share with you an "e-interview" I held with one of this book's previously mentioned case studies. As this part of her study will show, the interviewee is completely frank about her mixed feelings concerning writing ... but please, be sure to pay particular attention to her last response (now, do not cheat and skip ahead).

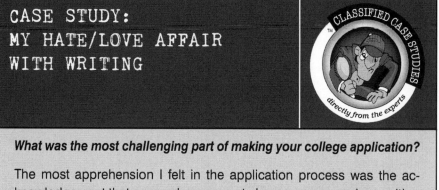

CASE STUDY:
MY HATE/LOVE AFFAIR
WITH WRITING

CLASSIFIED CASE STUDIES
directly from the experts

What was the most challenging part of making your college application?

The most apprehension I felt in the application process was the acknowledgement that my grades were not above average and my writing skills were below par. Despite the confidence I now have after several years' experience in college, I remember that writing the application essays was a very unsure and difficult process.

Knowing that you are among those who do not like to write (essays or otherwise), what is the most challenging part of it — and how do you overcome it?

There seems to be a block in my mind. When I look at a blank page or a blank screen, I become overwhelmed with anxiety. It used to be unbearable. Now, after having to write so many papers in college, it has become easier.

I find that initially, when having to write, it is good to sit down and discuss how you feel and what you are thinking about the topic with a friend or loved one. I find that it is easy for me to verbally describe my thoughts and feelings but challenging to put into print. After talking about the topics with people, I suggest writing down facts and ideas on the paper while even ignoring the lines. Afterwards you can elaborate from there.

Oftentimes, I have verbalized my thoughts and had someone else type them using my words. Later, I would go back and reorganize. In the beginning, you might need someone to help you put the thoughts together in a fluid manner. The road to writing does get easier. It will never be a walk in the park, but it definitely gets smoother. Even just having a study-buddy, mentor or warm body to be there physically can help you stifle the anxiety enough to write. Just write. Throw it all up on paper and edit later.

Pretend for a minute that you like to write, what gratification do you find, and what is your favorite kind of writing?

The finished product is the most amazing part. Handing over that complete work, knowing that I have completed a task is the most pleasing to me. I find that it is most gratifying and easiest topic to write about is my personal life experiences and inner feelings. They tend to be the most captivating samples, too.

Have you ever been rejected from an educational institution to which you have applied? Did you feel it might have had something to do with your written application?

Fortunately, this did not happen to me.

Have you ever had a composition instructor, either in high school or early college, who really "turned you off" to writing? How did he/she do this?

No, actually most of my instructors have tried to encourage and challenge me to be a good writer. I have simply disliked it on my own.

Have you ever had a composition instructor who helped you "discover" the rewards of writing?

It is plain and simple that I do not like to write. Although I have had wonderful instructors, it is an innate thing in me to dislike writing. I have distractibility issues among other things. While I feel as though that through my experiences I have become a better writer, I still do not like to write.

Do you feel that writing skills have proven important throughout your post-college life/career?

I am still in college. But my friend, Anna, who is a teacher, tells me every day how important writing is in her profession. She told me once that her superior would write emails that contained misspelled words, uncapitalized and unpunctuated sentences. It seemed to her that the message was taken less seriously, in addition to the status that is lost for someone who is being paid more than you and has to handle more official responsibilities. Plus, as a teacher you have to set a good example. You do not want to teach your students mistakes that will duplicate over time.

—Pam Lasko, Student, Wright State University

My reason for using this case study is several-fold: Here is a student who admits to disliking writing, yet who applied to three colleges (recall her story in Chapter 1?) and was accepted by all three. Here is a student who still feels that writing is not her "thing" and yet has learned how to successfully navigate the waves; and — most importantly — here is a student who grits and grinds her way through every essay assignment (I know this because I have helped with one or two of them), but who recognizes the value of making a good presentation of oneself through the written word, both scholastically and in the real world.

All right, then, let's start determining the degree to which your written application truly matters in the quest for admission to a college of your choice. Although I have already expounded (and will do so even more later on) upon the values of writing, the truth is, as in all things, that some colleges will hold this to be more important than others.

For example, a technical college such as the one attended by a future systems analyst will almost certainly not require the degree of writing skills equivalent to a liberal arts college application. The same goes many times for the college or university that focuses solely on the courses you have taken, your GPA, and your SAT/ACT scores. Nevertheless, the better the written application, the more appealing the student will look to an admissions officer, because strong writing skills reflect an overall ability to learn, grasp and — most importantly — disseminate and share information. Just as poorly written essays may make them think twice about their decision to accept that student. Even if your chosen career goal is to find yourself awash in systems programming and software design, do not forget that other students are hoping for the same career course and are applying just as you are. I feel quite safe in assuming that, even in such a techno-centric institution, writing abilities just might be the "tiebreaker," if needed, when it comes to making final selection as to which students will be admitted. Richard Lasko's case was unique, and he was fortunate not to have had to write an application essay, but you cannot count on that being the same for you. All other things being equal (such as GPA, achievements, extracurricular activities, and the like), the student who will be admitted to the last available position will be the one who can best express him or herself in that application essay that otherwise would not seem so important because there will not be an over-concentration of writing work done in pursuit of the degree.

Bear in mind, however, that when you graduate from Techno-Tech University, the expectation is that you will be able to perform amidst the circuitry (remember, you are a walking advertisement of a finished product), and that in the course of your professional dealings, there is a good chance that you may have to write memos or instructions to employers, fellow employees, and customers using your company's systems. Naturally, this type of writing is more of what is termed technical writing, but even the most basic technical writing will reflect upon you and your overall ability to do the job well. Rightly or wrongly, careless or haphazard writing reflects a similar perception of your overall capabilities — and those admissions officers at TTU will be able to see that long before your potential employers and clients in four years' time.

And, since I have strayed into the land of silicon, let's mosey back to the other side of the equation … the institutions at which strong academic writing talents are considered to be of utmost importance. Just to clarify, academic writing abilities are those normally thought of (and dreaded) when one thinks of college … the research, the formal quotations, footnotes and endnotes and work-cites (oh, my), the argumentative essays, and such — in other words, the "non-technical-writing writing." It goes without saying that the writing skills and the effort put forth in an application essay at Dartmouth will hold more weight than at TTU; whereas the application essay for the latter was a "tiebreaker," some colleges will use this essay as their first criterion as soon as minimum GPA, test scores, and other basic qualification requirements have been determined.

At this point, you may need some reassurance, and I will gladly oblige. You have been reading about all the trials and tribulations you are going to face and how you must excel and apply yourself and all that rah-rah intellectual hype. The bells are ringing in your head and the academic clock is about ready to chime. Yes, all that is true, but it is not an education death-knell; you are going to be fine.

In the first place, do not forget that you are a young adult entering a whole new phase of life and its attendant challenges. Colleges and universities recognize the importance of these trials and the need for students to adapt to new circumstances while honing abilities and strengths. They also want students to understand that higher education facilitates academic growth and excellence and also new forms of knowledge, and as a result, college will serve as a starting point for the professional career. Colleges and universities want you to work and study hard; but they also want you to enjoy the time that is spent there, to be involved in the many different organizations offered (perhaps not in the way of Uncle Joe so much); and it is imperative to discover how the college years will provide a strong, firm foundation for the future. Your job as a college student is to take those opportunities and develop them as best as you can into as many memorable and educational experiences as possible.

Of course, colleges want academically capable students; yet, they also seek applicants who possess a variety of well-rounded experiences, including extracurricular activities and community involvement. These activities might include team sports, volunteering, (see the case study near the end of this chapter), clubs, and part-time jobs. Fraternities, sororities, and other on-campus organizations will offer an array of social and professional networking opportunities; any combination of one or more of these experiences will serve a viable purpose in promoting a well-rounded individual with the potential for success throughout life, as well as helping to form life-long friends and contacts.

Your ability to expand upon your creativity and self-expression is also one of the most important challenges of the college years, and this process begins with the admissions essay. This essay allows you to summon your inspired energy and to demonstrate to the college admissions committee that you are serious about wanting to join their ranks. All of the things mentioned in the previous paragraph are worth remarking upon and may even provide some useful starter fluid for that creativity — if laziness does not dampen the charcoal.

Bear with me one second: another (Ms. Hahn) lecture is forthcoming here. You should consider yourself fortunate in that, with little if any exception, you will be asked to submit your essay(s) in typewritten form, and normally online. I once applied for a job advertised in a community newspaper that required a five-page personal *handwritten* biographical essay. When I called the potential employer to verify that this was not a typographical *faux pas*, the secretary assured me that it was indeed correct: "Mr. [Jones] feels that only people who really want the position will go to the trouble." (By the way, I did handwrite that essay, albeit quite tediously and messily from lack of practice, and got the job.)

And do not forget Ms. Lasko's case study, wherein she talked of having to handwrite and then typewrite all her college work? Many of you have most likely never even used a typewriter, where it was not so easy to delete and cut-and-paste. There was an excess of wasted paper and frustration; if one had somehow forgotten to insert a whole paragraph, and it was toward the beginning of a 15-page assignment … Believe-you-me, the amount of time required to do any kind of college writing has been significantly reduced in the past 20-30 years, and for that, you should be <u>extremely grateful</u>.

What I am getting at, though, is another example of how computer technology has both helped and hindered the college application process: the physical act of writing that essay has, without question, been made much easier with the advent of word-processing, and that encourages a certain amount of indolence because it all seems too easy. One drawback with submitting an essay online is that it is all too easy to click on "submit" accidentally, when you really weren't ready to send the essay in. So as in all things computer-wise, take care. Also, the work a computer does and the output it produces is limited to your willingness to channel your own creative energy onto those keys. Even with the best technology, laziness will show through. Quality in, quality out; garbage in, garbage out.

As I will cover in the next few chapters, meeting all the basic requirements we have discussed are in reality only the opening act for you to "strut your student stuff" to the board of admissions, and the real headliner will almost certainly be performed within the lines of a written application essay. We have already discussed that some colleges will consider standardized tests or overall GPA to be of more significance than others; your smartest bet, therefore, is to have done your best in both of these areas. Similarly, regardless of what type of school attracts your interest, a well-worded, thoughtful application essay to the college of your choice will bespeak your true desire to attend this — or any — educational institution. Even if there were some fully accredited Fantasy U that promised *never* to have written assignments (keep dreaming, dear reader), just to get into that Fantasy U might require a sincere and strong self-promoting essay.

On the topic of self-promotion, and in keeping with the reference made earlier to community service and volunteering, the following case study, written by a grad school colleague of mine who teaches in one of our city's most prestigious parochial schools, has this to say:

CASE STUDY: AN APPLICATION TO BE PROUD OF

As a high school English teacher for many years, I have helped a number of students write college application essays. At its most fundamental, the college application essay process is fairly simple and only requires students to be praising of themselves. The most difficult challenge is finding a balance between humility and self-praise. The student needs to laud his or her accomplishments, but at the same time make note of the fact that he or she needs the college to which they are applying to further hone their talents. This is a key element to the essay process. The student must show that he or she is able to be taught and desires such. If this balance is struck, then the applicant will be in good shape so far as the admissions committees are concerned.

In general, a good college-applicant résumé-builder is service work, or any work that deals with justice. However, this work should not be done just to pad that resume. A sincere devotion to justice (or lack of same) will come across in any college application essay. Sincerity is key; colleges want an honest and dedicated individual who can show he or she has committed to something for a period of time. Service work, particularly long-term, shows that an individual is committed and caring, which is a very attractive trait to any college administrator.

To bring things into a more personal perspective, I moderate a group of students, M.A.C.H. 1 (Moeller Advocates for Community Housing), who seek to provide affordable housing for Cincinnati's indigent. Working mainly in the part of town known as "Over-the-Rhine," I and my crew have stripped vacant and decrepit buildings down to their bare skeletons and then remodeled/refurbished them in order to give otherwise-homeless inner city people a chance to get off the streets and have a roof over their heads.

This experience is most helpful in preparing students for college, as it teaches them leadership, time management, and a myriad of practical life skills. Sending altruistic students to college betters the college campus and has a profound ripple effect on all whom come in contact with the student. Additionally, colleges look highly upon individuals with experience in justice work, as justice is the most honorable goal for which anyone can strive.

—Mike Moroski, English Department, Moeller High School

To conclude this chapter, and as is evidenced by the above case study, colleges and universities do not just seek students who satisfy their academic requirements; they also seek to *develop* prospective students and their ambitions. Obviously, students who are willing to get their hands dirty and help those in need already show promise as people who will apply themselves to any worthwhile cause — including themselves. If you can present yourself as one who is confident and willing to build upon that confidence during the educational process to further develop yourself all around, you will undoubtedly score high in the committee's favor.

Take note: an admissions officer, who is not there to help you learn or improve your writing skills (that will be done by your instructors/professors), will be looking first at the overall quality of your self-representation so far as it reflects you and not so much (at this stage) your writing technique, although — just as in GPA/standardized testing — it never hurts to do your best in both.

❧✦❧

Chapter 7

What Do They Truly Want to See and Hear in an Essay?

As I have begun to discuss, college admission requirements characteristically include the development of an essay, or series of essays, addressing several questions regarding topics such as personal career aspirations, strengths and weaknesses, and other related issues. It is typical to find several required questions, and also one or more optional questions, for consideration. Beware the application that has four or five essay type questions, but with a word count of 200 or so. You have only a few sentences to use in order to answer the questions, so be sure the few sentences are the best that you have ever written. As a college applicant, it is your responsibility to read these questions carefully and to determine how to address them in the most appealing way. Colleges accord positive evaluations to essays that are complete and precise, and those that are not too wordy or that serve as "filler" without any true substance. There are many books available that offer examples of good, "winning" essays (see the Bibliography), and you might want to read over at least a handful of the successful ones so as to get the "feel" of how these essays should work.

Although I have never been an admissions person, as a college composition instructor, I can guarantee you that it quickly becomes apparent which students are truly making an effort (despite some all-too-frequent technical issues) to express themselves well and which ones are too lazy or unconcerned to even make that effort. It is also readily obvious which students are going to wax on forever just trying to cover the minimum page length requirement. All quantity, no quality — embarrassingly evident to both writer and reader.

Perhaps the most important first step to developing a successful admissions essay is to remember that you are writing about yourself in your own words. You should not make these words so dull and bland that readers will find your story and life history the most boring piece of material on earth. On the contrary, you should recognize that your narrative is no less interesting or fascinating than anybody else's, and therefore you should develop your opinions and thoughts stimulatingly and creatively as possible.

You should also recognize that there are indeed limitations to the type and extent of information that you reveal about yourself in the essay (we have all heard the catch-phrase T.M.I. — too much information); yet, you should also realize that you must keep your concept appealing. Your words should be identified as a part of what you represent, and therefore you should disclose details that will sell your story to the admissions committee and that will promote a sense of understanding and empathy towards your character. You want them to read your essay and say to themselves, *Now this is the type of student who belongs at our college. He or she represents a strong character and will show a commitment to his or her academic studies.* This type of response to your essay is most desirable, and you must work hard to get to this point and to make your creation stand out from the rest.

In Chapter 2 of his book *On Writing the College Application Essay,* Harry Bauld offers a short dramatic scene of the endless fatigue and boredom experienced by college admissions officers as they plow through dull application essay after dull application essay. Although Bauld writes from firsthand experience and paints a wry and jaded picture, the fact remains that some of these students will be accepted and some will not. The importance of catching an essay-reader's eye cannot be overstated; though, you should not be led to believe or fear that unless you submit *Gone With the Wind,* your essay does not stand a chance.

Here is a good example, a case study written by a pharmaceutical major, which will then be compared to a distinctly different one submitted by a lifelong humanities college professor and author.

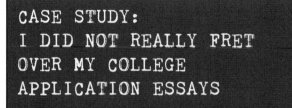

CASE STUDY:
I DID NOT REALLY FRET
OVER MY COLLEGE
APPLICATION ESSAYS

When I was applying for college, I sent written applications to Ohio State University, Ohio Northern University, the University of Cincinnati, and the University of Toledo. I selected these institutions because they offered my selected major, pharmacy, and they were all in-state schools.

To me, the most challenging part of writing any college application essay is coming up with content or a story that will really score with the college admissions team. The absolute most challenging part of making my applications was the random essay question, if one was required. I found it easier to be given at least some idea of what to write. I did not ask anyone for help, and in fact did not have any help with my admissions essay, unless it was with a dictionary or thesaurus or the like.

When it comes to impressing admissions faculty I would tell applicants to try to think of the best situation in their life that applies to the question. Do not lie or make up extraordinary situations to make yourself sound greater than you are. Just pick a normal example of whatever the admissions faculty is asking about — but it is always a bonus if you can throw in points about being a leader, service in the community, or some other good quality.

—Amanda Gray, University of Toledo

Now, let's hear from a completely different perspective:

CASE STUDY: HOW IMPORTANT IS WRITING TO THE DECISION TO ACCEPT A STUDENT AT A COLLEGE?

I believe the application essay is a crucial element in the acceptance process. All the data that students submit — grade point averages, transcripts, extracurricular activities, and so on — can be misleading, as the reader cannot be sure exactly what is being measured, or against what standard. Even standardized test scores tell more about the socioeconomic status of the student's parents than about the student's specific abilities.

But the application essay gives the college a chance to hear the student's individual voice. This voice reveals something about the student's verbal ability (though the reader must always allow for the possibility that the student has had help polishing the essay), but more important, the essay reveals aspects of the student which cannot be quantified — how the student thinks, how s/he perceives the world, what her priorities are, what values he offers to the college community. The essay, in other words, is a place where the student can distinguish her/himself from all the other super-achievers she is competing with.

Let me use as examples my three stepsons — three young men, all academically gifted, but with very different personalities and talents. They used their application essays to reveal something unexpected about themselves, something not to be found in their school achievements and extracurricular activities.

The oldest wrote about the shock he experienced when, in the ninth grade, he moved from a Montessori school to a traditional high school, where — in contrast to the more individualized assignments and process-based evaluations he had known for eight years — he encountered highly structured classes and frequent grades. It was quite a shock, and at first he was not very successful in this new environment.

But he used his intellect to analyze the new expectations and figure out ways to meet them, and soon he was as successful as his new school as he had been at his old one. This story revealed the struggles of a confident young man experiencing failure for the first time in his life; his success indicated his ability to face challenges. More importantly, the voice of the essay — self-aware, humorous, wry — offered significant information about the quality of his mind. Any admissions officer reading this essay would have a strong sense of this student as a person, more than any transcript or test score could convey.

The second young man traced his choice of academic specialty — Eastern Asian languages and cultures — to his encounter at 14 with an animated version of The Romance of the Three Kingdoms, an ancient Chinese novel about war and politics. The world revealed by the film so fascinated him that he not only read three different translations of this thousand-page work, but created a small club of like-minded students at his high school. His essay examined the values he found in this culture and analyzed how those values might provide meaning for his life in the very different context of modern American society. By focusing on a story unique to him, and by articulating the significance of this story in a voice unmistakably his own, he provided an admissions officer a valuable clue to the qualities he would offer the college.

The third, rather than focusing on his career goals of medical school, chose to write about an unusual achievement that he prided himself on: every day for the last two years of high school, he rode his bicycle to school, a hilly five-mile trip each way, carrying a backpack nearly half his body weight, and undeterred by any variety of inclement weather. This feat, and the motivations for it, revealed a number of important things about his character: his determination, his desire for independence, his concern for the environment, and his delight at being different from virtually all of his fellow students. His transcripts and test scores testified to his academic abilities; in the essay, he offered the admissions officers access to those other qualities a student can bring to the college community.

What each of these essays had in common is that they approached the assignment from an unexpected angle. Each young man chose to emphasize an aspect of himself other than academic ability or career goals

> to tell a story about who he was and where he was coming from, and in a voice that revealed the self behind the numbers (and each young man was successful in gaining admission to his first-choice school). That is what a good college application essay needs to do.
>
> —Kathleen L. Spencer, Ph.D

It is certainly a "no-brainer" to spot the differences between these two case studies, and they do reflect a good example of what we discussed earlier: the importance of writing can vary, depending upon which school and what type of college major you will decide to take. Although Ms. Gray has somewhat downplayed her effort, the truth is that a future pharmacologist/pharmacist will not be having to write on the same level, or style, as a foreign-language major (conversely, the foreign-language major will not have to memorize the periodic table of the atomic elements — or whatever that thing is that I could never make heads nor tails out of in science classes). But what these case studies do have in common is that all four of the students got into their schools of choice — and they all had to write that essay.

You can, too. Let's start to examine some of the fundamentals, most of which you have heard ever since you started doing book reports in grade school and which have been expounded upon right up through the present.

To start, decide upon your thesis (do not let that nasty word scare you — let's instead call it a "mission statement" if it makes you feel better) and what you intend to say to promote that statement. There is something you want to say, and a reason you wish to say it; all that should come through as your essay develops. By the end, you will have introduced, expounded upon, and concluded your mission, which has with any luck enraptured your audience and given them a clear insight as to your capabilities.

The beginning of your essay should not open with a lengthy, tedious opening sentence, because this type of introduction will get you nowhere fast — with the possible of exception of on the "reject" pile. If your reader has to look back and re-read several times just to get the idea, your essay is doomed; therefore, you must develop an introductory sentence and an opening paragraph that addresses who you are and what you represent as quickly as possible. Your readers should not have to backtrack, nor should they have to read two or three paragraphs into the essay to discover who you are and what you are about; they should be able to tell from that first sentence forward. If you develop a strong introductory sentence and paragraph, it is likely that the remainder of your essay will flow properly and will lead to a successful body and conclusion.

One of the more interesting experiences I had as a teacher was with a student whose literary skills were minimal at best, but whose essays were among the most powerful I ever read. Coming as he did from a rundown inner-city project area, his papers could have easily started off along this standard line (and taking the liberty of cleaning up spelling, punctuation, and such): *I always wondered what it felt like to be shot.* Instead, his style was a far grittier, eye-catching approach, which went along this vein: *Bang. I fell into the stairwell. My ears rang and my leg and side burned like hell. The concrete was cold. I tried to get up but felt numb.* Immediately, the reader knows or can infer much about the author; he has been shot, seems to be in a cold, tough neighborhood, and despite pain and numbness, has the presence of mind to try to recover. Compare this with the first selection, where all we know is that the author has a curiosity regarding bullet wounds. We do not know whether he or she ends up getting shot, or knowing someone who does get shot, and his/her curiosity truly does nothing to set him/her apart from most of us who, at one time or another, have almost certainly wondered the same thing. Naturally, this was a classroom essay and not one for an application, but the fact remains that this latter example reflects an author who is honest and wants to engage his reader by approaching the story from a far more interesting and compelling angle.

Some of the most common misconceptions regarding the college admissions essay are related to the need to be "safe" when writing this essay, rather than to demonstrate creativity to the admissions committee. In reality, where will being "safe" get you? Face it, without an interesting opening statement, your essay is likely to be destined for failure — a boring joke without a good punch line, and the admissions people are more likely to fall asleep, to go "Bauld," than anything else. Therefore, your first sentence and the entire first paragraph should represent you and your personality the way in which you want others to perceive you. You in all probability do not want to start out the essay with a side-splitting joke, but there are other meaningful ways to avoid a bland introduction.

Your opening statement should be authentic, demonstrating why you as a prospective college student would be successful at the school of your choice. There are countless ways to approach this, such as with humor, conviction, shrewdness, strength, or even sadness or fear; but regardless of the approach that you take, you must demonstrate that you are serious and sincerely want to take the next steps to obtain a college education. Your words are meaningless unless you write them from inside, from the heart, and you must continue to expand upon your thoughts and observations regarding the topic of choice throughout the essay.

You want to make your first sentence glow and appear alive as best as you can. As the old saying goes, "One does not get a second chance to make a first impression," and therefore you must write to impress the first time. A creative and catchy first sentence and subsequent paragraph will lead you down the appropriate path through the remainder of your essay. Yet, if you feel you must start with a "safe" first sentence, follow it with a catchy phrase or statement that will attract the reader's attention: *I always won-*

dered what it felt like to be shot. Friggin' curiosity be damned — it hurts like
hell and I cannot move to tell them not to throw me in that ambulance.

This process is not rocket science, and frankly, it is not that different from writing an essay for a high school English class. You have just served up an appetizer and salad for your audience; now, the meat and potatoes of the essay must be strong and filling, followed by a dessert that leaves a good taste and satisfaction in the reader's confidence in you as a student. You have been hearing this recipe throughout your schooling, and have most likely been doing so even subconsciously as your writing skills have grown and improved. Or, to look at it in a more verbal way: when you tell a story or relate an incident, you try to first catch your listener's attention, hold it throughout your narration, supply whatever details are necessary, avoid straying too far off course, and then hope to receive a satisfactory response when you are finished.

I know there are many of you who simply do not believe you have the talents to do this in writing something, but I beg to differ. Allow me to share another teaching tale, because, after all, most of my students were the same age as you and were just beginning college.

Along with the three major essays that were due in the term, I asked my students to write a paper depicting the first time something had happened to make them realize the world was not necessarily as "safe" a place as they once thought. In my generation, the first such instance was the day John F. Kennedy was assassinated; I was only six years old, but can vividly recall that day (better than I can recall what I had for supper last night); I know where I was in what classroom and who the teacher was and what she wore … you get the picture. In my students' generation, many of their first such moments were the *Challenger's* fatal launch, the Oklahoma City bombing, and of course 9/11. One student even wrote about Hurricane Katrina, because as she explained, she was able to resonate/identify by seeing the impoverished people *as individuals* clinging to rooftops far more than just watching buildings fall or planes crash into fields with countless unseen casualties. This was an interesting observation and perspective, and certainly made her essay stand out.

Anyway, this particular assignment was optional and for extra credit, but I offered it for the following reason: many of the students would come back, completed papers in hand, flat-out amazed at how smoothly the writing had gone. Even some of my most recalcitrant writers, despite the less-than-happy topic, actually enjoyed the act of expressing themselves in writing — for the first time ever in their school life.

The reason for all this ironic optimism-amidst-disaster was, of course, that the incidents and all the details had already happened, and as such their minds did not need to "start from scratch" when it came to finding a place to begin. *I was lying on the couch, almost asleep, and I opened my eyes just in time to see the plane hit Tower 2 ...* — or, more catchingly — *Almost awake — Wow, what a movie! The special effects are terrific — awesome! Uh, oh ... wait a minute, wait a minute, something's wrong ...* Drawing upon something that had in reality struck emotional chords, they truly revealed a great deal about themselves and their characters in that particular essay; some were not ashamed to admit they cried, and others talked about how much they suddenly realized how much some people in their lives meant to them — and how much they meant to others. There were those who talked about feeling angry or hopeless, and wishing they could be there to help. Finding a starting place for your application essay in actuality should not be too difficult. You certainly must have some strong memories and preferences as to the aspects of yourself you wish to share or embellish upon to meet the established criteria for admission. These characteristics should start to be seen right from the get-go: the introduction. (Again, I defer to the works — and others — in the Bibliography; if you take the time to check into one or two of these, you will soon see that every success-ful application has begun with a strong introduction, and the many ways to achieve this).

Let's assume that you have written the introduction of your life in develop-ing the college admissions essay. It is not too wordy, it is creative, it is heartfelt, it is funny, and it describes your personality to the proverbial "tee." What happens next? How do you follow through and keep the re-mainder of the essay strong? Believe it or not, you have a number of op-tions that allow you to develop an essay body that will suit you perfectly. The first step in this process is to remain focused. Without a clear focus, your essay is likely to go off track as quickly as it began — just as when you verbally relate a story but allow too many side comments. This kind of derailment is fatal, as it is often incredibly difficult to go back and figure out just how or why you jumped the rails in the first place. Therefore, you should do your best to develop the body in the same way you developed the introduction: with a little flair and finesse. Your commitment to the essay in its entirety is what will get you through the writing process staying on track and keeping your message clear.

Because you have already established a specific tone during the introductory portion of the essay (with which you are especially satisfied), your best bet in completing the essay is to hold that voice throughout the remaining paragraphs. If you continue to develop your work with the same tenor and style, your attention to the project will be obvious to the admissions committee, and they are likely to view your essay favorably. These paragraphs might be looked upon as the DNA that holds the entire body together; if you have not lost your focus and continue on the same voice-path as the introduction, your demonstration of well-directed and controlled creative energy remains strong, thought-provoking, and sincere.

A good example can be found in the wounded-student essay previously described. There is a powerful, attention-grabbing introduction, but the tone and voice of the essay must remain consistent throughout. In case you are a little unclear as to what I am saying here, reread that opening. In your mind, think of the typical old black-and-white detective movies, wherein the narrator speaks tersely and pulls no verbal punches: *Bang. I fell into the stairwell. My ears rang and my leg and side burned like hell. The concrete was cold. I tried to get up but felt numb.* The speaker is abrupt, to the point, and maintains a sort of sarcastic sneer that echoes in his delivery and choice of words.

No matter how brilliant that introduction, that essay would have been ruined, shot through the heart, and fallen down into the stairwell right along with its author, if he had suddenly decided to try to sound intellectual or soft-hearted: *I found myself thinking about my beloved Angie, and how she had always begged me not to come down this street after dark. Oh, how I wish I had listened.* This not only "clashes" in the reader's ear, sabotaging the picture that is already been formed of the author's character, but also shows an inability to stay on the course that has been set.

After you have written the introduction and body of your essay, you should conclude your work as it began; often, it is good to round off with a mirror, or complementary nod to the introduction: *"I will never wonder again what it feels like to be shot; I now know."* (the first example) — or, and much better: *"My leg's still sore and I have lost some blood, but what the hell — I will live."*

I have already cautioned against trying to be too funny, but if you began the essay with a humorous note you should conclude in likewise fashion. This approach will at least prove that you are consistent and that, in spite of the essay's humor bookends (intro and conclusion) you have taken your mission seriously. On the other hand, if you wrote the essay with a serious tone, do not end it with a joke or a lighthearted comment. Again, the attitude of the essay should remain consistent throughout — right up through the final punctuation mark. In many ways, the conclusion is as important as the introduction, as it more or less wraps things up, and also may be what the committee most retains.

If your essay tells your life story or a specific phase of it, end on a high, positive note, accompanied by a few statements that reaffirm who you are, what you represent, and how you might develop and grow from the college experience that you are seeking. This optimistic approach is likely to have a favorable impression upon the admissions committee and should work well for you. And please, no wimpy, ingratiating, and obsequious, *I hope that college will turn me into the ... I want to be;* you are certain that college — especially this college — will do that for you. Fawning and "sucking up" are easily recognized and sternly frowned upon. Also, when writing about "why" you want to attend a particular college (if that is one of the questions), do not write *I want to be a (mascots name) because my family has followed your football team forever;* as this is a sure way not to impress them either. Believe it or not, this has been used in many unsuccessful essays.

If you have adequately researched the college to which you are applying, you will know what will and will not work for this specific institution, and can write your essay in such a way as to show the board you would make a good fit into what they stand for and what they consider to be of high priority. The following case study reflects one student's experience with having to write an applications essay for an incredibly selective private school.

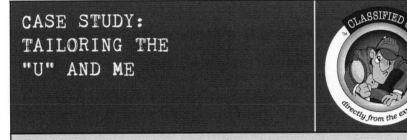

CASE STUDY: TAILORING THE "U" AND ME

A part of the application process for undergraduate admission to many universities is the submission of an application letter of intent. I have always understood that this process helps you to differentiate yourself from others in the applicant pool. I attended a small private liberal arts school in Austin, Texas. St. Edward's University did require an application letter, which at first made me feel nervous, but after discussing the subject with my parents and some of my favorite teachers I knew exactly what I needed to write. My academic record was going to speak for itself and it was up to me to show the admissions committee who I was and what I was going to add to the student body at St. Edward's.

St. Edward's is a Catholic institution, so it probably did not hurt that I had attended Catholic school most of my life and could play up in my letter my desire to attend an institution that had a vested interest in my "moral" development. I also focused on all of the extra-curricular activities that I had been involved in, sports, volunteering, etc., and also touching on what I wanted to achieve through the college experience. I discussed the value my parents had always placed on education and how both my grandfather and my mother were educators-turned-principals.

Further, I am sure that I dropped in a quote from Walt Whitman or some other transcendental poet who valued individualism, the "real" zeitgeist of America, and all its other dreams and promises of success. All in all, I figured it was just one more hoop that I had to jump through, but that if I could pull it off it would help my chances of getting in to a great private school. (At the very least, it would show the admissions people that I could write in complete sentences, conjugate verbs, and that I could even properly use a semicolon.)

Thanks in part to my solid writing skills and education, both at St. Edwards in Austin and Xavier University in Cincinnati, I am now working for a grant-funded project and will be performing a lot of administrative coordination work, along with editing, writing, and communication, marketing, and public-relations material.

—Christina Burke-Tillema, M.A.
Aligning Forces for Quality, a grant-funded project
through the Robert Wood Johnson Foundation

As the above case study can attest, the author was able to utilize aspects of her life that she knew would be considered to be of importance to the college of her choice — without fawning and "sucking up," but playing on the truth and strengths she knew would help her cause. She developed a powerful essay centered around those aspects, and the end result was, indeed, just what she had hoped for — admission into St. Edward's.

COLLEGE APPLICATION

Chapter 8

~~~❖~~~

You Know What They Want, but How Do You Prepare to Write This Thing?

ear Abby:

At this time of morning, the attic is pleasant-ly cool and the pile of rolled-up sleeping bags I am propped against smells fresh from Mom's dryer. She always washes the bags before she stores them up here until our next camping trip. She is downstairs making breakfast, and just called up to me, which is fine because it will get too hot in another hour, and I am not getting anything done anyway. I came up here because it is peaceful and I need to start my college application essay, but the legal pad in front of me has nothing but scratch-outs and a few doodlings. (If you look close, you can see the imprints on this page because I tore off the first one.) Do you have any suggestions about how I can best go about this?

—Signed, Desperate and Deadlined

Depending upon your creative abilities and strengths, you might view writing and the writing process as an evil monster lurking under the bed — or the soft fresh-scented sheets on top into which you can snuggle and let your imagination flow. For many students, the actual thought of writing is perhaps the most difficult part of the academic career, while others look forward to the chance to show their ability and stretch their creativity as they work toward fulfilling the college dream. Bear in mind that the monster lurking under the bed is more frightening to imagine (because he does not in reality exist), and that once you force yourself to crawl out from the comfort of those sheets and take a quick peek below, you realize that you have wasted a lot of time fretting and stewing — just like the ACT/SAT. Well, this is similar. Yes, unlike the nonexistent, creature, the need to write a college application essay does exist, but the longer you let your fears and imagination build up, the more terrifying this process will be.

It has been a couple of chapters since I mentioned my least-favorite p-word; perhaps it is time to reiterate the Perils of Procrastination, with a little help from my co-author, whom you may find more credible simply because, as she readily admits and unlike me, she *is* one:

Procrastination is the root of all evil: just ask me!

I was born, raised, continue to be, and will die a procrastinator. My ability to put things off is uncanny, and it often amazes me how well I do with things when I have sufficient time to perform them. If you are at all like me, you possess a strong tendency to postpone things until the very last minute. You may stall and stall some more until there is no time left. As a result, your focus may be limited, in addition to your time. Take my advice: do not procrastinate on the college admissions essay. If your application is due on February 1st, do not wait until January 30th to begin writing the essay. This is not sufficient time to complete the essay and to improve your chances of admission to the college of your choice. If you do so, your essay will be glaringly weak to the admissions committee, and they might even deny admission on the sole basis of your creative weaknesses. This unfortunate circumstance could be avoided with a time, effort, motivation, and perseverance.

I will be incorporating some more of her thoughts and suggestions in a final chapter, but for now, I want to make sure to dissuade you from letting that presumed under-the-bed "writer's block" become the counterweight for Big Ben (the clock in London, not the Pittsburgh Steelers' QB). The

longer you put things off, the more easily this can happen.

And trust me, it does not have to be so. Do not think you have nothing of any worth to write about and that *Nothing interesting has ever happened to me;* Bull cookies. At this age and stage of your life, you have more than enough material at hand; you merely have to organize and present it in such a way as to make an admissions officer take notice. You no doubt have had many experiences in common with other students, but also many more that are unique to you alone.

For example, the morning after my 16th birthday, I awakened at about 5 a.m. and something told me to look out my bedroom window … just a quick, kinda-voice in my head said: *Look out the window — Now.* For whatever reason, I obeyed — just in time to see and hear a massive explosion down the street. At first, I thought it was a house, but as it turned out, our newspaper man's van had been rear-ended by a drunken driver. Clay, a rather large man with a roly-poly build, somehow squeezed himself out his rolled-down passenger window (the collision had jammed the station wagon's doors) and escaped with mostly 2nd-and some 3rd-degree burns. The next time he came to our house to collect the bill (several months later), it was the first time I had ever seen him without his trademark cab-driver-type cap, and his bald head was horribly scabbed. Clay continued to deliver papers — in his brand-new station wagon — for several more years, but he could never wear his beloved cap again, as his scalp remained too tender after various skin grafts.

At first glance, this story seems real innocuous (at least so far as writing an application essay is concerned), but think about it: if I had been wondering how to write an eye-catching, unique essay, this might have been a good place to begin … I am sure many other 16-year-olds had witnessed fires and seen people who had been in accidents (or have had the misfortune themselves), but this was my event, experienced from my perspective, and the whole eerie experience of being told to look out the window just at that precise moment was, in some ways, the beginning of a new revelation to me — if for no other reason, the sudden awareness of just how fragile life can be and how quickly things can change in a split second.

To this day, 34 years later, I cannot explain it, but there was a definite reason for this incident, and I can still hear the phantom voice directing me to sit up and take notice. Had this been someone else's experience, he or she might have recognized it as the beginning of the desire for a medical career (or the main reason for never wanting to deliver newspapers). Still another student, after seeing Clay's resulting injuries, may have taken it as the moment he or she decided upon a legal career, specializing in personal injury. On a more spiritual side, it may have called another student to religious studies, as whatever powers that be must have had Clay's back that morning. In any event, this unusual experience would have made an outstanding "hook" — one that would certainly make an application essay more noticeable than others.

We have already talked about attention-grabbing and "hooks," and the sample winning essays found in some of the reading materials listed in the Bibliography will be able to offer more ideas along those lines. For the time being, I would like to concentrate on the most fundamental problem at hand, which echoes the chapter's title: *How do you start to write this thing?*

Let's face it — whether or not you like to write, you are highly unlikely to sit down in a position of uncontested power and immediately pound out a masterpiece knock 'em dead-flat-on-their-butts admissions essay; you are far more apt to stare at a blank computer screen or legal pad for hours on end with no creativity in sight. Right now, before I go any further, I would like to offer the first and foremost of many pre-writing "tips" I can share with you regarding work such as this:

☞ *It is never a good idea to just sit down and expect to write — especially something of the magnitude and importance of a college applications essay.*

A Kroger list, yes; a quick email to your best friend, yes — but not anything that requires serious concentration and has a real, lasting purpose. Long before you physically sit down to take keyboard or pen in hand, you should be thinking and strategizing. You might do well to keep a small pocket notebook (more about that in a moment) at the ready for those occasional *aha!* thoughts — those unexpected flashes of inspiration as you ride the bus or mow the yard — because the worst thing you can do (in my humble but well-proven experience) is to just sit right down, cold turkey, and expect to wham-bam produce a good, solid essay, unless you are one of those rare people who have a natural flair for writing and can actually sit down and put pen to paper at the drop of a hat.

I realize that many of you would prefer to keep notes and lists electronically, and this is certainly fine, but when considering writing an essay, the value of a 50-cent pocket notebook can prove immeasurable. It is portable, convenient, and requires no plugging in or recharging. When an unbidden thought comes — out with the pen or pencil, and there it is; the notes are always visible and do not need to be "accessed" or downloaded. Plus, I have found that normally, just the physical act of handwriting — opposed to pounding keys — will allow an idea to stick more firmly and thus have a better chance of being built upon. The notes do not have to be neat or legible to anyone except yourself — if you are truly struggling with the idea of writing an essay, I doubt they will ever be worth a small fortune because you have become a best-selling author and they have been preserved for posterity — but hey, you never know.

Whether or not you actually use any of these notes is of no consequence; the main reason for this suggestion is that creativity tends to build on creativity, and you might be surprised to find how many thoughts start to flow once you have begun to jot down even just a few of them. Some of the notes will seem trivial and meaningless, but anything you can pen down along the lines of forethought will more easily attack that blank computer screen or legal pad when you sit down to begin serious writing. The important thing is to start searching for ideas before you start drafting the essay and allow yourself enough time in advance to let an essay gradually take root.

For what it is worth, even creative people can often find their creativity to be a challenge. Peter Illyich Tchaikovsky, the famous Russian composer, once said something along the lines of: "It is the duty of an artist never to submit to laziness ... one cannot afford to sit around and wait for Inspiration; she is a guest who comes only to those who call her." I do not recall where I first read that quotation, but I do recall it was on the back of an album cover and — fledgling author that I fancied myself to be — I copied it down on an index card and slid it under the glass top of my desk for those times when I was ready to say, "Screw it; I cannot think of anything to write." In retrospect, these were times that I plopped down in my chair and just expected the ink (no computer in those days) to flow and flow, all on its own — and that just flat is not gonna happen. Without the medium of your imagination and the willingness to invite inspiration, the ink will remain dry.

In other words, even the most creatively gifted student will need to seek out some ideas and think ahead before sitting down to write that application essay. It would not surprise me to learn that Tchaikovsky had some sort of pad upon which he might scribble some musical notes that would eventually find their way out from his pocket and into The *1812 Overture* — and some that did not. What I would be extremely surprised with — no, I would not believe it at all — would be to learn that he wrote the whole piece (which is awfully short by classical music standards) in one sitting. His work was no doubt a culmination of long thought-process and diligent effort; the genius is that the final work sounds so easy — as if he tossed it off one Saturday afternoon just before dinner.

All right, enough about Peter Illyich; what else should you do to go about preparing for that final moment when you sit down and begin drafting your essay? Here come pre-writing tips No. 2 and 3; you may or may not agree with them, but I, and many of my students, have found them worthwhile.

☞ *Set a begin-time/date and stick to it.*

Although the note-taking process can be lengthy and may even continue as you work your way through the drafts of your essay, have a definite target begin-date set — one that allows you plenty of time to meet your application deadline — and hold firm to it. Barring an emergency, you should have a time cast in proverbial hourglass sand that will mark your first assault on the monster/keyboard/legal pad.

Let's define *emergency*: illness/accident requiring unexpected surgery for you or an immediate family member, the house burns down, there is a tornado warning, and power outages last all weekend (but even at that, you could start writing by hand).

Now, instead, let's define *emergency-not*: a last-minute party invitation, a chance to go on a river boat ride, a co-worker wanting to change shifts (for non-emergency reasons — see prior sentences), your headphones broke and you need to shop for new ones, you stayed out too late last night, the weather's excellent for shooting hoops down at the rec center, your best friend Eric just got a new car, Jenny's cat just had kittens, your printer ran out of ink, there is a wonderful movie on HBO, you would rather nap ... this is another instance where I could elaborate for the next ten pages (and by the way, all these plus many more are real student excuses I have heard for not turning in work on time). Yes, this can be humorous to an extent, exasperating to an even larger extent, but in the long run; these excuses-not can be completely destructive toward a successful college career.

The bottom line is that parties and boats rides and hoops and cars and kittens aside, college work will require discipline, and this is as good a place as any to start. Tell your friends and co-workers that you will be unavailable on X-day beginning at X-hour and working through X-hour. If they are the kind of friends you should truly have, they will be understanding and will not interfere with the time you have stated ... but, as an added precaution, you may want to turn off that cell phone and not log onto the net while you are beginning your work. This way, the potential for distraction should be significantly diminished.

You are also much better off and more likely to see positive results if you set aside the time, if possible, as the first thing in your day or the first thing to do when you get home from school or work. Whether you are an early riser or get up just in time to see the break of noon, the essay's time-slot should be at the head of your day's to-do list. By first going to see Jenny's cat's kittens or Eric's new car, you are inviting distraction and the awful p-word, thus courting disaster. Once you are at Jenny's, it is easy to decide to go down the street to McDonald's *(I will get something to eat now so I do not get hungry while I start working on my essay)*; with Eric, a quick jaunt down the local interstate to show the car's power might turn into a day-trip to the next town *(I will think some more about the essay while Eric's driving us back.)* It does not take too much imagination to see how one thing can easily lead to another, and ***poof!*** your day is over, with nothing having been accomplished.

Before continuing to my next "tip," I should assure/reassure you that I do not believe this initial work on the essay should be lengthy. I am not suggesting that you hole up in your room for an entire weekend, or even all day Saturday or Sunday; but a good two to four hours should suffice to at least get you to take a quick peek under the bed and see the monster is not in reality there — or, at the absolute least, it is not as fearsome as you imagined.

I am also not suggesting that you must <u>wait</u> until your designated start date/time; if you should become inspired before then, by all means, go for it. Strike while the iron's hot. Grab the bull by the horns. (So many old adages, so little time.) Again, though, if you decide to sit down and make that all-important first effort, turn off the electronic distractions and give yourself a better chance of staying focused.

Now, back to pre-writing "tips":

~~~~~~~~~

☞ *What about outlines?*

Why did I not mention them yet? I have not done so for two main reasons:

(1) My personal experience with outlines has never been helpful, and therefore I almost forgot to mention it. In truth, as much as I love to write,

I have never been able to discipline myself to the practice of outlining …
perhaps it is too mathematical, too structured? I honestly do not know;
though, I can say that I was never able to stay within the boundaries of an
outline — they tended to start taking a life-form of their own and all of a
sudden, I would realize that I have done at least as much — if not more —
writing than in the essay itself. What I did find, though, is that once the
first draft was finished, I could go back and outline *ex post facto*, and that
would help me to see if my thoughts and the resulting paragraphs flowed
smoothly. I simply could never do it in advance. (I am sure there are many
English composition teachers out there right now who would love to have
a "private chat" with me, but that is just the way it is.)

(2) YET, having dispensed with the truthful item #1, and maybe to ap-
pease some of those aforementioned English composition teachers, I now
say that if an outline works for you, by all means, do not hesitate to use
it. You may have already been forming it in the notepad, your phone, or
wherever you are keeping track of possible ideas, and there is absolutely
nothing wrong with the technique — unless you allow it to actually hinder
your progress. Do not get so "hung up" on the outline that you find yourself falling behind in the actual start-of-essay process; to invoke yet another
old cliché, this would be a classic case of "the tail wagging the dog."

Yet another "tip": I firmly believe that, at this stage of things, you should
not change topics unless there is a good enough reason to do so. By now,
you have been spending at least a couple of weeks (if not more) thinking and note-making and preparing for X-day/time; a subject should have
begun to take form, though hazy, and it is counterproductive to suddenly
decide that another topic might be better. In essence, you would be starting
from scratch, and bear in mind, although you have (with any bit of luck)
allowed yourself plenty of temporal leeway, time has a way of passing very
quickly and deadline is upon you.

By the way, this is <u>not</u> the time to read those other successful essays I mentioned earlier here and also in Chapter 7. All that will do is throw you into a virtual tailspin-tizzy. With any luck, you did the wise thing and checked out at least some of them prior to now, because to do so at this point will only add to the confusion. The preliminary thoughts you have had, while looking good in that notebook or in a computer file, may suddenly seem trivial, incompetent, or inconsequential — in a word, *booooorrring*. (I feel safe in stating that I seriously doubt you will suddenly feel any new confidence in what you have been planning.) Yet, as always seems to be the case, there is a "but;" if one of those sample essays truly struck a chord with you and you had been planning on using it as a model, you may want to re-read it to refresh whatever it was about that particular one — but please, stop there. Do not risk adding more confusion or losing your confidence by reading more essays.

Before we move on, and since we are talking about reading other people's works and possibly emulating them when writing our own, there is a second naughty p-word you have almost certainly heard many times before, but it is worth repeating now: *plagiarism*. **DO NOT DO IT.** Recall that if you do incorporate someone else's work (and in a personal essay such as this, that incorporation should be minimal if at all), you <u>must</u> put quotation marks around the "borrowed" words and give appropriate credit wherever it is required, depending upon the recommended style — for example, in a footnote, endnote, or on a works cited page. If you do so and stay within the boundaries of reasonable borrowing, you are not plagiarizing.

But at this stage of college writing, you may not want to borrow at all, because citation can get messy. The essay author, essay title, and the author/editor and title of the book in which it appears should all be mentioned, in whatever format is recommended by the admissions board. As a hypothetical example, you may have incorporated a line from the following: "The Inveterate Tailgater" by Joseph E. Williams, reprinted in *Twenty Successful Application Essays from THE Ohio State University*, collected and edited by Seymour Brewskies, Ph.D, Dean of Admissions and printed by the OSU Press, 2007. It is easier (not to mention less time-consuming) to just stick to your own words; there will plenty of time for academic writing in the next two-to-four years.

One last reminder: do you recall the chapter in which we discussed how modern technology has, paradoxically, both helped and hindered modern-day higher education? Perhaps better than any other, the topic of plagiarism offers a well-sharpened two-prong paradox in that although students can avail themselves more readily of literally countless essays, articles, and the like via the web, teachers, administrators, and admission board members have the same — and many more — options to do so, as well. In case you have been playing 21st century Rip Van Winkle lately, there is software dedicated exclusively to helping educators ferret out suspected acts of plagiarism. And even without the sophisticated, state-of-the-art technology (which not all institutions can as yet afford), that same sentence or paragraph you Googled into your essay can easily be Googled out from even this least highly-advanced, and therefore most accessible, search engine.

So, to wrap up this chapter, here is another instance of guaran-damn-teeing you: Google in, Google out — and you along with it; forget about attending college. At least this one, if not all of them. Presumed lack of creativity, laziness, and the hopes of not getting caught are not worth the price you may end up paying; although your admissions essay may not be an "award-winner," it can certainly be the proverbial *coup de grace* that ends your college dreams, and for reasons far more severe than simply being "boring" or "typical."

Plagiarism: DO NOT DO IT.

Dear Desperate and Deadlined:

The way I see it, you are well on your way to writing that essay. You took me right up there to that attic with you — without overdoing it — and I can tell that you come from a loving, supportive home. It sounds as if you are giving yourself plenty of time, or else you would be sitting at the computer trying to pound out some last-minute "any ol' thing will do" essay. Just hang in there and relax; you will be surprised when that moment of Inspiration strikes — because you have invited her — and the words start to flow. Best of luck, and keep me posted.

—Abby

P.S. I do have six words of advice:
    Do not procrastinate, do not plagiarize.

Chapter 9

Some More Grist for the Preliminary Writing Mill

*I*n Chapter 7, I mentioned that different colleges have different requirements regarding the application essays. Some questions may be incredibly basic and require some third-person observation on your part: *If you were a newcomer, how would you describe your hometown?* Some questions might be more introspective: *Please describe your strengths and weaknesses in better detail. What would you define as your greatest strength? What is your greatest weakness?* — or — *Name the person who has provided the most influence in your life to date. What has this individual taught you about dedication and perseverance?* Still other questions may seem ludicrous: *You are delivering pizza to a new home in an exclusive neighborhood, and the customers (male and female) answer the* *door in the nude. What do you do?* — or — *If you could be any famous animal in history, which one would it be, and why?*

Although it is tempting to continue with the "ludicrous," there is still much ground to cover, so we had best move on — but maybe we can still use that second example once again. Along with knowing what your college of choice considers to be priority, one of your duties as an applicant is to find out the nature of the questions that you can expect from each institution and prepare yourself accordingly. If you are applying to a variety of schools, you may be required to answer the same series of questions more than once, even if they are worded differently from one application to the next. You may need to "tweak" an essay to make it a closer match to the re-worded but, in essence, similar one of another school: College A: *If you could be any famous animal in history, which would it be, and why?* is very closely related to: College B: *You have a choice to be Robert E. Lee's horse, Traveler, or Roy Rogers's horse, Trigger. Which would you be, and why?*

College A's question does not limit your choice of animal to be a horse, and it offers a wealth of imaginative leeway (no pun intended). College B's question not only narrows the field to horses, but further limits it to only two and leaves virtually no wiggle-room for spontaneous creativity — for instance, an applicant to College A might write that he would like to have been the Trojan Horse (especially if he is applying to University of Southern California), but if an applicant were to respond as such to College B (the University of California, Los Angeles, the cross-town rival of USC), even the most well-written Trojan Horse answer would suggest to the admissions officer that this student is either not paying attention or too lazy to write a second essay.

Make no mistake; admissions boards are often keenly aware of the questions asked by others, particularly of schools that are geographically close and therefore tend to receive applications from many of the same students, so do not be surprised if an admissions officer recognizes your ploy.

Now, what you realistically could do in a situation such as this is write to College B's question in such as way as it also answers College A: Of all famous animals in history, you would most like to be Traveler because even though he was on the side of the losing Confederacy, he never let his master down and was there from Bull Run (Manassas) to Appomattox. Or, you might like to be Trigger, because when he died, Roy had him stuffed by a taxidermist and put on display in a museum, so he truly "lived on," in a manner of speaking. This dual-purpose response is an honest approach; however, you must make sure that a multi-school reply meets each school's particular criteria, and this should be done before you sit down to truly begin the writing process. I hesitate to bring this up, but … after all, you may have to write more than one, and if that is the case, your preliminary thoughts and notes will reflect as such — right? But just as quickly, Valerie Lasko, whose case study is shown in Chapter 5 and who introduced the applications essay for us, confirms the less-arduous theory: "As I recall, I tried to use the same essay for each college application, but changed/tweaked it some based on each college's question." As her case reveals, she was accepted into all five colleges to which she applied; she obviously did a good job of writing/tweaking, according to the individual institutions' questions.

One word of caution: The more creative of applicants may be tempted to have some "fun" with these questions, particularly those that borderline what seems to be ridiculous, but this is not the time to strut your comedic editorial stuff. It is crucial that you take this part of the application process seriously, as it is a critical means of improving your position as a prospective applicant. What <u>would</u> you do if someone answered the door naked? Act maturely and professionally, hand over the pizza box, and politely look elsewhere while awaiting payment? Burst out laughing? Point and giggle? Start removing your own clothes? Scurry away in abject horror? Your college acceptance may be dependent upon a thoughtful and introspective essay as a source of promoting a strong case for admission; there will be time for literary mischief and BS (and I am not referring to a Bachelor of Science) later on. Some writing courses will actually encourage a bit of humorous writing, and perhaps the campus newspaper has a column space for you — but let's first get you into the school before we investigate those possibilities, unless you want to be a career pizza-deliverer.

We can take a time-out and regroup for a minute here; if all this preamble and warning and such are making you edgy again, let's return to the fundamentals — and maybe some more reassurance. Let's start with the fundamentals:

If you possess at least a basic set of writing skills, with an abundance of thought and a little bit of creativity, you should be able to develop and write an essay that will impress the admissions committee. Their evaluation of it will require them to assess not only your writing skills, but also to make a strong effort to understand you as a person. This will not be accomplished without your own concerted effort, which requires you to produce an essay that will not only impress the committee, but will also invite them to see the "real" you. Colleges and universities are undoubtedly interested in your academic strengths and weaknesses; yet, there is increasing pressure on you as the applicant to demonstrate your own character and personality. Your essay's thoughts and words be clear and free of grammatical errors and typos, and provide the committee with a basic understanding of your talents, abilities, and personal traits. Your capacity to write a thoughtful essay may make the difference between an application that teeters on the fence rail between admission or denial and one that will lead to a successful outcome.

And now, the reassurance, which I will present in the form of another case study written by a young woman currently working on her doctorate — and who (as you will see), has never felt truly "comfortable" with writing. When I asked her to contribute to this project, I suggested that she submit something that would reflect the way in which she might have written her first college application essay if I were the one-woman board of admission to the K. L. Hahn College of Advanced Writing:

CASE STUDY: I WRITE EVEN WHEN IT IS WRONG

I think this has to be one of the more difficult pieces of writing I have had to do — writing about writing. It is akin to discussing the importance of breathing or blood circulating throughout the veins. How much time can you spend talking about why you must breathe or why blood must move around throughout the body? The necessity of those two functions is so obvious as to preclude a prolonged discussion on the matter.

I am writing my PhD thesis in Economics and also working as a full-time college instructor in Economics. To get to this point, I've written my way through high school, college, and graduate school whether it be in English classes, on exams, for papers in different classes or comprehensive exams. I've been taught how to write more effectively, I've learned by doing and I've adjusted my own writing style to avoid what I dislike reading in other works.

I cannot survive in my profession without writing. On the one hand, I need to write for professional publication, which requires one tone or style. On the other hand, I need to write in the course of teaching, which requires a completely different approach. Most students are unfamiliar with Economics and the language of the discipline turns many of them away before they can be comfortable with the field. I've found that re-working the more sophisticated writing into more everyday language smoothes this transition and allows me to then use the formal terminology with a greater degree of success.

However, to put it mildly, writing is not always my favorite activity. The most difficult aspect of it is putting into words what I want to say — I usually have a general outline of the topic at hand, but I often write a sentence, delete, write a sentence, and keep that but delete the next one. Rarely do the thoughts and words flow in a seamless fashion. I work hard for every paragraph. These difficulties aren't as pressing when I am writing for lectures, but they are exacerbated in non-academic writing. This is true even when I am writing in a diary! I've never even seriously attempted fictional writing because story ideas or characters just do not pop into my head.

Overall, I write best when I am passionate about something, but even then the aforementioned issues still rear their heads in the process. I love the idea of writing, just as I've always loved the idea of running or skating. The latter two I can work on to get better, but I think that the difficulties I have in the writing process are simply a part of how I work, and will always be there — but I am usually quite happy with the finished product, which is what really counts.

—Katharine (Katie) Kontak, Economics Instructor
Bowling Green (OH) State University

Obviously, the mythical KLH College of Advanced Writing would never refuse to admit a PhD candidate, but all that aside, the "admissions essay" Ms. Kontak wrote would be considered interesting, insightful, and revealing as to the potential student's personality and abilities. She begins with an interesting conundrum/comparison, winds through the body of the essay detailing what and how she has had to write thus far, admits to her shortcomings, and ends on a positive note. She does not try to over-flatter or overstate her desire to do what this hypothetical school will no doubt require (write, write, and write some more), but her approach on the whole bespeaks of her determination to work hard, improve, and achieve.

And let's not forget her obvious major interest of study; unless one is turning out articles for *The Economist* or similar publications on a regular basis, writing will often step aside for mathematical formulas and economic models. In other words, she is by no means one who aspires to write for her living, but she has apparently done well thus far and impressed the real universities (University of Massachusetts and Bowling Green) to which she applied, both as student/grad student, and faculty member.

The whole point of this is to remind you, once again, that even though writing may be a challenge for you, many who share your same discomfort have found their way through, and even — by golly — *improved* as they pursued their courses.

Okay, fundamentals and reassurance have been dispatched, so let's move forward with another suggestion or two about preparing to write that essay, beginning with an ergonomic angle: where, or in what kind of environment, do you think you would be most comfortable writing? Is the old familiar computer desk in your room the best way to go, or should the notebook (electronic) or notepad be carried somewhere different, just for a change of scenery that might in turn lead to better Inspiration? Hmmm … this reminds me of something that happened to me in (I think) my eighth-grade year; again, I ask you to bear with me because — believe it or not — there is a point to my sharing it with you.

Most of you are too young to recall, but you may have seen in TV reruns, the long-running family show "The Waltons." (Yes, I can see the eyes rolling upward and hear the collective sigh — but hear me out.) The show's storyline was of a family struggling through the Depression and World War II, but its main protagonist, John Jr. (I won't say "John-Boy" because you are already impatient and making faces and tapping your feet), had only one career goal in life: to write. In one of the more memorable shows, the family home catches fire and burns, swirling John Jr.'s almost-completed first novel manuscript up to that wonderful cinder bin in the sky. The young man is understandably devastated, especially because he saw the pages burning but could not get to them in time — and because he thinks his pipe smoking may have caused the blaze. Even after the house is fully repaired, he cannot seem to rewrite or even begin to rewrite the work, and he almost surrenders his dream of writing for good.

But, as in all such shows, there is a happy ending. One day, tired of trying to resurrect his book from the mental ashes of despair while sitting at his new desk, John packs up his writing tablets and pens, makes a sack lunch, and hikes off by himself to sit on a huge boulder by a rushing mountain stream ... and lo and behold, he finally begins to rewrite the novel that would eventually be published.

So ... one day I, as a nature-loving fledgling wannabe novelist (but for the immediate moment, an English student who desperately needed to write a most-elusive essay of her own), took spiral notebook and pens — and some potato chips — and headed for a bare-trickle that passed for a creek a short distance from my house. As you can imagine, what worked magically for John-Boy on TV did not perform the same miracle for Kathy-Girl; not at all. The breeze kept flipping the pages; the sun's glare was too harsh; I could not get comfortable on even the largest rock; mosquitoes, gnats, and no-see-ums stung me in anatomical places I did not even know I had; forehead perspiration dripped onto the paper and made the lines run (there were no words, just the blue lines); hand-sweat smudged things even worse; and my potato chips spilled all over — which was okay, because the ants had already infiltrated the bag, as I had learned when one stung my tongue when I bit into the same chip it was eating.

(Can anyone say *reality check?*)

All right, the John-Boy/Kathy-Girl story's over; you can stop groaning and pay attention again. The reason I shared that with you is to forewarn that if you have given some thought as to going somewhere totally different to begin your writing, please check it out first indoors or out, but particularly the latter — whether you are taking laptop or pad of paper, can you sit comfortably, and a find a position amenable to typing or writing by hand? Is there enough light? Are there restroom facilities (besides the nearest tree or bush) nearby? Is there shelter, in case the weather turns? Is it the season for annoying insects? Will there be a plethora of other people around — and therefore crowding, or creating a huge potential for unwanted noise and disturbances? Any or all of these factors, if not determined and prepared-for in advance, can lead to — you guessed it — an unexpected delay that sabotages your best-laid plans to begin that essay. For sake of convenience, you may be better off just staying put in your customary work area, but there truly is something to be said, especially if creativity seems evasive, to going somewhere else, even just for the start of your project.

Now, hand-in-hand with ergonomics, which in essence refers to the physical comforts of your writing arena, we must also discuss atmosphere. I should have mentioned: when discussing ergonomic/physical concerns above, that to each individual, there is a unique preference. For instance, one of my best friends in high school liked to write while lying on her back, head propped on a pillow, right ankle crossed over left bent knee, and with her notebook propped against the crossed-over leg. With her extremely pale skin, she looked like a raw pretzel, especially because she was left-handed, but it worked for her (not for me; I tried it several times). The same goes for atmosphere, and I again go back to a previous paragraph: maybe the noise of a crowd would not disturb you as much as it might someone else. The key to all of this is being able to set your surroundings according to what works best for you along the lines of artistic comfort.

Many people — especially younger people — like to have heavy-metal, rap, or hip-hop (I hesitate to call any of them *music*) blaring as they work; others prefer silence. Some students like to have the TV on, even if they have no clue as to what is actually going on, let alone what program is showing. Although I certainly have my preferences, I realize that silence or real soft music does not work for everybody; there is truly no "right" or "wrong." The important thing is to get that essay underway, and it is up to you to set the appropriate atmosphere that works for you (which is, of course, more easily accomplished in the familiarity of your room or special study area).

The last thing I will touch on before we get into the writing itself (in Chapter 11) is to make sure you are prepared and well-stocked so far as materials are concerned. Everything that we have discussed in the latter part of this chapter has concerned itself with issues that will continue to be important even after you have been accepted and begun your college career, and this is no exception. Whenever you sit down to begin a writing project — especially if it is one that seems to be a bit challenging, try to ensure that you will not have any unnecessary materials-related interruptions.

This includes, and in fact is led by, the fact that you should always be sure to have a backup printer cartridge handy. In our modern-day dependence upon the computer and printer, there is nothing more frustrating or potentially debilitating or derailing as running out of ink in the middle of a project. I realize that at this stage, we have only been talking about preparing and getting ready to begin writing, and you may not even think you will need or want to print at this stage, and you may not need too. But trust me: always having a spare, new cartridge is a critical element for success in college, and this is as good a time as any to get into the habit. Paper, pens, notepads ... these always seem to be nearby and "scrounge-able," but that certain-numbered ink jet (or laser) cartridge can be quite elusive at the last minute (even if the stores are still open), so be prepared. Printing has another value too. Although your essay might be submitted online, having a hard copy can have its value, too. You may want to print an unfinished copy to take with you and add to on a whim if needed. It is also a good idea to have a copy of the essay for someone to proof if they do not like to do that on computer (as some of my teachers refused to do). You can also read it over if needed yourself, no matter where you are and do not have to depend on having a computer to do so. Lastly, if you have a last minute interview with someone from a college, or if you just do not have access to a computer at the time, a printed copy of your final work comes in handy to go over before the interview, as some are done after they have received your application and some questions might be based on that.

I once had an overachieving student come to class with a half-printed, ink-fading-fast, due-that-day essay. He was absolutely frantic, and I was afraid that even at his young age, he was going to have a heart attack right then and there. "Ms. Hahn! Ms. Hahn! The printer ran out of ink just one page short — it always runs out of ink in the middle of printing — never any-time else."

Well, *duh*.

It also goes without saying that you may not need to print anything right away; finishing what you wanted to accomplish today and saving your work will suffice until you can get that cartridge replaced. That is fine; I concede that Rome did not fall for want of a single full ink cartridge. In fact for some applications you may not need to print anything at all, as more and more, applications are being done entirely online.

But the real lesson to be learned here, and since we are closing on the chapters regarding preliminary considerations, is that being prepared might be the Boy Scouts' motto, but more importantly, it is also the college student's (or college applicant's) salvation. Preparation in the form of knowing what is expected and when it is expected, preparation in having tried to lay some preliminary groundwork in the form of notes and outlines, preparation so far as knowing where you will be most comfortable and likely to summon your best creativity and preparation in materials — all of these will contribute positively not only to the success of your application essay, but for many more writing assignments to come. Unlike procrastination and plagiarism, this is a *good* p-word.

And now, before actually talking about the act of writing itself, and in case you are still floundering about for a thesis (mission statement), Chapter 10 is devoted to helping you stir up some possible ideas for your essay. These are in no way, shape, or form meant to be the theses (statements), but they may jump-start your mind into thinking of a direction that might not otherwise have occurred to you. If you already have a good, strong topic in mind, that is cool; skip to Chapter 11 if you so desire. For the rest of you, let's check out 10.

Chapter 10

Some Possible Essay Thought-Starters

*A*gain, please note that most of these are not meant to be thesis (mission) statements, or the whole thrust of your essay; they are merely for brainstorming purposes and to maybe help you think along some lines you might not otherwise have done.

Categories

Animals

- Do you have pets or have you spent much time around animals?

- Have you ever had a favorite pet?
- What have you learned from animals?
- Do you have career interests involving animals?
- What is your favorite zoo or circus creature?
- What is your favorite show or movie about animals?

Athletics

- Do you participate in athletics? Or did you want to participate and were unable to for some reason?
- What is your favorite sport, either to do or watch?
- How do you feel about the amount of money that athletes make?
- Have you ever suffered a serious injury while participating? If so, how has that impacted you?
- Do you feel that today's "trash-talking" and "in-your-face" type of play is healthy competition or poor sportsmanship?
- Are there any athletes you truly admire or dislike? Why?
- Do you think that professional athletes are setting good examples or should set good example for today's youth?
- How do you feel about athletes who are arrested, caught cheating, or doing something else that is illegal (steroid use, gambling)? Should they be banned from their sport, or how many "chances" should they be given?

Careers

- If you had a "dream job," what would it be?
- What is your idea of a "nightmare job"?
- How important is it to you to like what you will be doing?
- How does income play a role in your career choice?
- What do you see as the biggest challenge facing someone just trying to break into the workforce?

- Do you think you would make a good supervisor/foreperson/ manager? Why or why not?
- What was your first job? What was the most important thing you learned from it?
- How do you envision your retirement?

Community

- To what sort of community do you belong?
- Do you participate in any community affairs or projects?
- What do you most like/dislike about your community, and why?
- If you were "in charge" of your community, what would you do to change it for the better?
- Can **one** person make a difference, and if yes, how?

Current Events

- Do you keep yourself apprised of what is going on in your community, the country, and/or the world? How do you do this (TV news, radio, newspapers, and the like)?
- Within your lifetime, what do you think has been the most significant issue (global warming, failing world economies, and such)? Or had the most impact on you?
- What do you think has been the most "much ado about nothing" issue?

Dreams (when sleeping)

- What have been some of your most memorable dreams?
- Do you think dreams hold any special meaning?
- Can dreams foretell the future?
- What are some of your recurring dreams? What are the common themes?

- Have you ever been able to solve a problem in your dreams that you were not able to solve while conscious?

Entertainment

- What is your favorite TV show, and why?
- Do you enjoy going to the movies or staying home with Netflix?
- Do you enjoy live pop-music concerts?
  The symphony/opera/ballet?
- You are any famous TV or cinema personality.
  Who are you and why?
- Do you enjoy watching older shows, shows that originally aired before you were born? Why or why not?
- What kind of restaurants interest you the most
  (Not just the food, but the ambiance as well)?

Families

- How would you describe your immediate family (the people with whom you live)?
- How would you describe your extended family?
- If you are an only child, have you ever wished you had siblings? — and conversely, if you have siblings, have you ever wished you were an only child?
- Of all of your relatives, living or dead, who has had the most positive influence on you, and why?
- If there are any deceased ancestors you have heard much about, which of them would you most like to meet, and why?
- What are your future aspirations as to having a family in the next five or ten years?
- If you choose to have children, what do you think will be your biggest challenges as a parent?

High School

- What has been your fondest memory so far of high school?
- What has been your biggest challenge thus far?
- Which teachers are you most likely to not forget the longest, and why?
- What has been your most embarrassing moment?
- What activities have you participated in and enjoyed?
- What is one thing that you would do change your school?
- What is something you wished you could have done differently (such as participated in more or less sports or clubs, or other activities)?
- What do you think accounts for the current disturbing trend of violence in high schools? How can we reverse the trend?

Historical Events

- What, in your opinion, has been the most significant historical event thus far in your lifetime?
- If you were to become a famous historical figure, how and for what reason would you be like to be remembered?
- Do you believe that spirits "haunt" historic places, such as (for example) Gettysburg?
- When you read or think about history, is there any particular place and/or timeframe that truly interests you? Why?
- You are on a famous historical ship. Which would it be, and why?
- What historical person would you choose to meet and why?

Hobbies

- In your free time, what is your favorite pastime? How, when, and why did you first get involved in this activity?
- Do you often share this hobby with others?

- Do you feel the hobby may eventually become financially lucrative?
- Has the interest in one hobby led to others?
- About how much of your spending money goes toward your hobby?

Lifestyle

- How high do you rate the priority of material wealth?
- What is your favorite vehicle, and why? Are you more of a compact, pick-up, SUV, or Corvette-type?
- If you could own or live in any kind of residence, what would it be like?
- It is Friday night and you have a date with your girlfriend/ boyfriend and seemingly unlimited pocket money. What do you do?
- Next Friday (because you spent all your money), you have a date with her/him, but you are flat broke. What do you do?
- Do you find it comical or disturbing to see the extent to which some people will go to hide their age or change their appearance?
- You are given the choice to keep only one of your technological "toys" — will it be your computer, cell phone, X-Box, or — ?
- Do you find it interesting to keep up with the social antics/legal problems/marriages and divorces of celebrities?
- What do you think of TV reality shows?
- You are getting married, and are ecstatic about it. Is a fancy, expensive wedding important?
- You are stranded on an island and may only take one item with you; what would it be and why?

Music

- What is your favorite kind of music, and why?
- Is there any particular song or musical composition that has special significance to you?
- If you could play any musical instrument, which would it be, and why?
- What is the first song you can ever recall hearing?
- Do you enjoy singing, either alone or in a group?
- Has a particular lyric ever truly "moved" you?

Nature

- What is your favorite/least favorite season, and why?
- What force of nature do you find most fascinating or frightening? Do run-of-the-mill thunderstorms frighten you?
- Would you rather be on the beach or in a forest?
- What is your favorite kind of body of water, and why?
- Have you ever seen an especially beautiful sunrise, sunset, or snowfall? Describe it and how it made you feel.
- What you think when you see the moon and stars?
- Do you like to "see" things in the clouds?
- When deciding upon a place to live in the future, how does the environment play a role and why?

Religion/ Spirituality

- Do you believe in a Higher Power?
- Do you think that religion can be harmful?
- Have you ever had what might be termed an "epiphany" — a moment of spiritual truth that changed the course of your life?
- Do you believe in life after death?
- Do you believe in spirits or ghosts?

- Do you lend any credence to spiritualists, mediums, or parapsychologists?
- Do you think there is any truth to the "near-death" experiences, where people declared clinically dead have been revived and tell of their "adventure"?
- How big of a role will your choice of religion factor in your life or your family?

Social Issues

- What do you think is this country's most pressing social issue, and how should we address it?
- To what extent have we (the United States) overdone, or do we need to do more, to help social issues in other countries?
- Have you ever felt especially moved by seeing someone mistreated, socially abused, or neglected?
- Is it possible to overcome stereotypical attitudes, or is this an unavoidable side of human nature?
- Do you think that prejudices have gotten any better than in the past? Or is there a way to peacefully combat prejudices (race, religion, ethnicity, sexual orientation, bullying, etc.) in the world today?

Travel

- Where would you most like to go, either in this country or another, and why?
- What is your favorite mode of travel?
- Are you afraid of flying?
- If you have traveled anywhere in your life, where has it been? What do you most recall about it?
- You are going on a cruise: is it the Caribbean or Alaska?

- If you could live in any foreign country, which one would it be?
- Do you think you would ever enjoy doing out-of-country service work, such as the Peace Corps?
- You have an opportunity to go to Niagara Falls (which you have never seen). You may do this in the winter, when many of the attractions are shut down for the season, but it is not at all crowded and everything is dirt-cheap and the Falls are beautiful if it snows. Or, you can go in the summer, experience everything, but get jostled and pay out the butt to stand in long lines in scorching heat. What is your pleasure?

Scenarios

Read and respond to these as honestly as you can; bear in mind, no one else will see them; it is just an exercise for further self-reflection and — again — a possible good self-brainstorming session.

- You are walking down a city street, and see someone running your way, being chased by a police officer. What do you do, and why?

- You are driving alone on a country road late at night and accidentally strike a dog who has wandered onto the road. The dog is obviously hurt, but is not dead. What do you do, and why?

- You are in a restaurant, or some other public place, and see paper money falling out of a man's pockets when he stands up. You cannot see the denominations, but there are obviously more than a few bills lying on the floor. Unaware, he starts to leave; do you let him know, or is it "finders-keepers"? Why?

- While at work, your boss compliments you on something you did not do (it was another co-worker, whom you in reality do not like, mainly because he is a real slacker). How do you respond?

- A longtime friend has truly hurt your feelings; you are upset and incredibly angry. How do you react?

- You go to someone's house to do a small "handyman" repair around lunchtime, and without first asking, they bring you a plate with some food that you are not allergic to, but just do not like. What do you do?

- You are in a fender-bender — the other (extremely apologetic) driver's fault — and you both do the right thing and exchange insurance cards. Your car is damaged, but not severely, and you are more shaken than injured. The next day, you feel okay physically, and the insurance company calls to assure you the repairs will be covered. The day after that, an attorney calls tells you there are grounds for a lawsuit and that you might recover a good-sized settlement. What do you do?

- You have found a cat and taken him in. He is affectionate, friendly, well-behaved, and fits into your household as if he had been there forever. Your own cat likes him; they are constant companions. A month later, you see a "Missing Cat" poster, complete with a photo that leaves no doubt. Why do you, or why do you not, contact the owners?

- While sitting in your classroom before the bell rings, you overhear two students behind you whispering; it is obvious they have concocted a way to cheat on the exam. Do you find a way to let the teacher know, and if so, do you do this before or after the exam? Or do you just approach them instead?

- You are doing some exterior painting for cash, and you suffer a catastrophic injury when you fall two stories off the ladder. It is nobody's fault but your own, yet the law says you can sue the homeowners simply because the accident occurred on their property. Do you? Why or why not?

- Despite your parents' strict forbiddance, you are at a party clear across town with your best friend. He is far too drunk to drive; it is after midnight, and you have not had any alcohol, but your first driver's license does not allow you to drive with anyone other than family members at night. No one else seems willing to help you out; they are either wasted themselves or refuse to go that far out of their way. You have no money for a cab and the buses are finished for the day. What do you do?

- You are a clerk at a small, independently owned hamburger stand in a rough neighborhood. A man comes in and demands you empty the cash register. He does not appear to be armed, and the store owner, whom you in actuality like and who has been good to you, keeps a handgun under the counter. What do you do?

- You accidentally take home a teammate's gym bag, which looks exactly like yours. Upon opening it, you discover packets that you realize contain an illegal substance. How do you handle this?

- A 16-year-old long-time friend has run away from home. With your reluctant permission, she has told her mother she is spending the night with you; when the mother calls and asks to speak to her, you panic and — without truly thinking — say "She is in the shower," and the mother takes your word for it. After hanging up, you are extremely guilt-stricken; do you call the mother back and 'fess up or preserve your friend's trust in you? And if you do call the mother back, what do you say?

- Your school tuition will amount to just under $40,000. You have found out you are compatible with a wealthy older cousin who desperately needs a kidney transplant. You have been offered $40,000 — do you take advantage of the offer? Why or why not?

- You find a wallet filled with money, but no credit cards or ID. What is your course of action? You find the wallet <u>with</u> credit cards and/or an ID, what is your course of action?

- You witness a two-car accident, and it looks as if there might be injuries, but you are already running late for the third time this week and your boss has said she will fire you if there are any more instances — and no excuses will be accepted. The job pays decently and will help pay some of your college tuition in the fall. What do you do?

- You are a high-school female, at a good friend's house, and her father makes an unwanted and uninvited "pass" at you. You discourage the attention and avoid anything further, but do you tell your friend about it?

- You are walking through a public park, and there is an elderly woman sitting alone on a bench, looking lost and ready to cry. What do you do? Does your response to this change if the sad person is anything other than female and elderly?

- In a grocery store, you see a young mother spank (not beat) her misbehaving toddler on the rear end with her open palm. She only spanks once, but another woman begins to scold her, and quite harshly. What is your reaction?

- You have read through these lists: did anything grab your attention or start a new course of thought? Which one(s), and why?

OK, that last one was just meant to be funny, but I do hope that not only did something jar your creativity, inviting Inspiration to come on in, but also that you have noticed every category and scenario leads to an "open-ended" question, which demands more than a yes or no answer.

Now, I am going to give you another real head's-up when it comes to college curriculum: even if the all-pervasive *why* is not included in every question, as is the case in some of the listed ideas above mainly because it gets so repetitious, you must <u>always</u> assume (unless told otherwise) that a mere *yes* or *no* is not going to suffice. Just for example, take a look at the second-to-last scenario: *Yes*, or even the high school-enforced complete sentence *Yes, I tell my friend that her dad made a pass at me is not sufficient.* The key to what is being sought is more the *why* of the answer than the answer itself.

I will leave you with one last thought … a good percentage of the above situations are things that I personally experienced (although I will never admit to which ones; I will leave it to my readers' imagination), and many of them occurred while I was in, or even before, high school. What this should tell you is that, as I have already stated but must now repeat, please do not think there has never been anything worth talking about in, or using as a main part of, your application essay. And in truth, especially so far as the scenarios go, your responses will give you and your audience a fairly good idea of the kind of person you are and what you consider important, either ethically or morally, in life.

Chapter 11

Ready, Set, Write (Phase I)

X-day is finally here. The day you have marked down as the beginning of your application essay. The day when the paper you are working on does not have pre-fabbed questions and lines for the answers or checkboxes for choices — in other words, the paper whose filling is <u>solely</u> up to you. The day whose output will help change the course of your life. The day you have both dreaded and anticipated because books like this one make such a to-do about it all.

All right; in case you have not noticed, it is X-day. For sake of argument, I am going to assume that you are well prepared.

For at least several weeks now, you have been seriously thinking about this, making notes, reading other students' successful essays, deciding where the best place would be to "set up shop," and you have reminded your friends 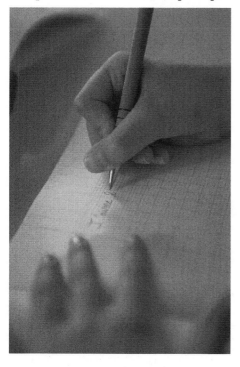 that you are off-limits from X-hour to X-hour. Just to make sure, you have turned off your cell phone and have resisted the urge to log onto the web (word-processing does not require internet service). And no computer games, either; you must stay focused. You have all the necessary materials gathered — your notes, dictionary and thesaurus, and enough paper and ink in case you decide you need or want to print something. You are locked and loaded, ready to rumble, at the starting gate, or whatever the current expression is to indicate that you are on the launch pad with all systems go.

At this point, I should step back and remind you that any of the writing "tips" I have already shared or will share in this and coming chapters are in actuality just suggestions. The best example of this is our discussion of outline or no outline; what does or does not work for me may or may not work for you. If it seems difficult to distinguish a suggestion and a direction when reading how-to books such as this one, you can strip it down to the most basic explanation: you <u>do not</u> need to follow any of my suggestions; however, you <u>do</u> need to write that essay as required. This might sound superfluous and unnecessary, but I cannot tell you how many times a student would walk into my comp class without a completed assignment: "But,

Ms. Hahn, you said [to/not to] do [whatever the 'tip'], and that just threw me off-track." *Sorry, my dear student; we discussed all that during class (and if you had not been so busy text-messaging your buddy across the classroom, you might have understood better), and the complete assignment is due today.*

Now that we have made the distinction, for our purposes here, I will offer two initial suggestions — both of which may actually surprise you. The first comes from something an instructor for whom I worked as an assistant once told his class of freshman honors students: **Lower your expectations.** That is right — you heard me, but before you take that too literally (and thus incorrectly), please let me explain:

One of the most serious impediments to writing is that feeling of having to produce something of the magnitude of, let's say, J. K. Rowling. You are no Rowling, nor are you Harry Potter; there is no magic that is going to set in and make you the world's greatest essayist. The first time I heard this instructor say "Lower your expectations" to his class, I was as stunned as the students, but the more he explained what he meant, the more sense it made. By the way, this instructor had heard it from a professor when he was working toward his Master of Fine Arts degree; that professor had heard it from one of *his* mentors, and that continued down along the line. It is only natural, when you sit down and want to do the absolute best work you have ever produced because this essay has been accorded so much importance, to set a degree of self-expectancy that perhaps even Rowling herself could not achieve.

On the other hand, the expectation level you should set is (as always) to do your absolute best. This is not unreasonable for anyone. You should expect yourself to make a concerted effort to produce an essay that bespeaks of a commitment to succeeding in college and a willingness to work hard to attain that success.

The second initial surprising recommendation I am going to make is to stop once you have gained some momentum. That is right; you heard me — but again, a more full explanation is warranted before you pick up that cell phone or log onto the web. To start off, by "gaining some momentum," I do not refer to having written two consecutive sentences. What I mean to say is that if the writing does begin to flow, let it flow and flow — but try to stop at a good place, a place at which you will be able to pick up where you left off and continue with much less effort.

Let's use the following scenarios to explain the reasoning behind this strategy.

Most of you, at some time or other, have worked on projects — whether it be for school assignments or something you enjoy doing as a hobby. Plus, in almost any venture, there will come a time or stage of that mission in which you run into a snag, or some sort of problem that you just cannot seem to resolve at the moment. Now, granted — sometimes this happens because it is late at night and you are tired, and the whole thing will look differently in the morning, but for the sake of our immediate scenario, let's assume that the glitch seems truly insurmountable … how much time do you spend dreading having to go back to that project, knowing what you are up against?

Conversely, how do you feel about returning to that work, when things have been moving along quite well and you know what the next steps or phases are going to be? You can think about it and actually look forward the next writing session, rather than losing sleep and worrying whether you will be able to finish successfully or even on time.

Along this line, when you one day join the professional ranks, you will find your weekends (or whatever is your designated time off) are much more enjoyable if you leave work on Friday with projects either completely finished or waiting to be picked back up on Monday at a good, manageable place. There is very little else as frustrating or demoralizing to leave on Friday afternoon with something hanging over your head … and yes, as I said before, perhaps you are just weary from the long week and Monday morning will bring a fresh approach, but many a weekend has been hampered by the dread of what is waiting for you on Monday or Tuesday (and trust me; it is even worse on a three-day'er).

This can also be true of writing, especially if you are one who has been struggling with the thought of this essay and dreading X-day. If you do find yourself moving along — and you stand a much better chance of doing so if you have done all the prep-work we have discussed — try to stop somewhere that you will anticipate coming back to the essay's first draft with a positive feeling. For whatever it is worth, this has always worked for me, whether I am working on a simple homework essay, a master's thesis, or short stories and novels — and many of my students also found this "tip" to be especially helpful. In some ways, it is similar to how you might feel all day knowing that you are going out for your favorite pizza for dinner; you anticipate and savor. On the other hand, leaving on a bad note can be likened to knowing you have a root-canal dentist appointment immediately after school or work, and dreading it so much that you cannot enjoy your day at all.

All right, let's try one other possibility on for size: suppose the essay truly takes off, and you do not want to stop because you are feeling so revved up about what is appearing on that monitor, and your creative engines are running smoothly ... do I still suggest that you stop? No. Work as long as you can — even all the way through, if that happens ... but do not forget: you are only finished with the <u>first draft</u>. More about that later. For now, let's stay on the momentum-related options and theories.

I suppose the best way to encapsulate the notion of when or if to stop can best be delineated as such:

- ➤ If you have been working away and gained some momentum but know there is no way in Hades you are going to make it all the way to the end today, find a good place and stop.

- ➤ If you even begin to suspect that you are coming to a "real" speed bump, slow down and stop before that bump grows into a concrete median barrier. In all likelihood, you will find the solution much more easily if you do not let the problem take on gargantuan proportions (like the monster under the bed) overnight.

- ➤ If you did think you could make it to the end, but find yourself flagging down the homestretch, finish the sentence or paragraph and stop (this would be a classic indication that you are just tired; you will be able to pick right back up next time with little or no problem).

- ➤ If you have been sitting for hours on end and nothing has happened ... no; that is not an option after all your prep work and pre-thought. Fuggidaboutit.

➤ If you make it all the way through that first draft, stop right there and give yourself not only a pat on the back, but also a good 24 hours before you return to the essay. <u>Do not</u> begin to proof or re-write — and that, by the way, is a *direction*, not a *suggestion*.

As you will note, in each of the bullet-points above (except the fourth one, which does not count), time plays a key role. Regardless of how little or how much of this essay gets written on the start-up date, an appropriate amount of time must be factored in before the actual completed project is ready to be submitted online or sent off in that application packet. Therefore, once again I remind you to avoid the first p-word, procrastination. Allowing for some healthy cooling-off time must not be read interchangeably with "putting off." Even if you got off to that unexpected absolutely fantastic start, do not assume that this means you can slack off; the job still is nowhere near complete, and time is passing.

All right, I have led off with a couple of broad ideas about this first attempt on the essay; you have been convinced to lower your expectations and to know that it is okay — and sometimes even preferable — to stop in midstream. Now, let's talk about some more specific "tips" that may facilitate your work at this stage … and do not worry; I am now back to suggestions. Some of you may find these helpful, and some of you may already have your own way of dealing with the things I am about to discuss — but it never hurts to listen (or in this case, read on).

➤ To begin, you are certainly aware of the admonition to save, save, save your work. To that I would like to add: save, save, save on your hard drive, and save, save, save to a backup — usually a USB-port "flash" or "stick." It also never hurts to send it in an email as an extra save, as I have had more than one flash drive quit working. Do not forget to remove the storage device from your computer when you are finished; if there is an unexpected power surge or other major catastrophe, the device can be fried or otherwise ruined right along with your CPU.

➤ Do not waste time or let yourself get bogged down by the occasional "speed-bump" of trying to find the exact right word. This is one of those bumps that can become a concrete barrier if you let it — but it also does not need to be one that encourages you to shut down for the day as discussed in the prior bullet-list. There are several ways to keep this bump manageable: type in the "almost-but-not-quite-right right" word and highlight it. In a later stage of the essay's development, you can always thumb through the thesaurus if that right word has remained elusive.

➤ Similarly, if you type in a word but the spelling in reality looks strange, the dictionary (not spell-check, which I will discuss next chapter) consultation can wait. This is another case where a highlighter will do nicely.

➤ Although highlighters are good for one-word corrections, I do not recommend you use them for everything (your first draft may end up looking too colorful, as if it suffers from yellow fever). For example, you may come to a point where you know there is something more you want to say, but you also recognize that you are just not able to think of that right now, and again — before letting that particular speed bump grow — simply mark the place and continue on. When I was teaching, I often read essays written by even my best students in which there would be an obvious gap between thoughts … the essay would be reading along quite smoothly, then *WHAM*, and then back to smooth the rest of the way. When I would make a note of this or bring it to their attention, the invariable response was "Dang [or worse], I wanted to say something else about that, and I guess I forgot it." These would be students who diligently proofread their work (I will also comment more on that next chapter), but the gap just never got breached. To avoid that (and after having had it happen to me more than once in my own writing), I suggest making some odd sort of notation, such as ++++++ or %%%%%%, anything that would tend to stand out as you re-read your work. (This also makes it easy to do a Ctrl+F search for those gaps when you start your re-write.) You do not want to use something basic such as "need more," because there is the off-chance that "need more" is used as part of your actual text, and the Ctrl+F cannot distinguish between what you meant to have in there and what was otherwise intended as a red flag tucked amidst the yellow words.

➤ Another trick I have learned over time is to set up a "dummy file" (no comments, please) into which you can dump some of your writing that may seem "not quite right" and yet, too good to just delete altogether. There may be a paragraph or sentence that sounds particularly solid, but just does not belong where you are right now ... for instance, you might be working on your introduction and suddenly think of an absolutely perfect way to end the essay. Rather than do the "lazy" thing and just hit ENTER a few times, you would be better off cut/paste-preserving that ending in your dummy file, because by the time you finish your essay, you may not recall 1) that the line is still there, out of sight on the monitor but further down in the document or 2) that you even wrote it at all.

➤ Finally, when you do decide to stop for the day, wherever you are in the process, try to leave yourself "briefed" as to where you intend to pick up — with what idea you intend to continue and where you hope to go with it. Do not make the mistake of thinking *Oh, sure, I will recall what I am going to say next* — it is far too easy to lose the train of thought once you have made an overnight stop at the rest station. Make notes to yourself on a separate piece of paper or maybe just type them in using a different font at your stopping point, and then close up shop for now.

You have done well today, and you are finally starting to see some results for all the hard preparation and over-thinking and over-fretting you have been doing these past few weeks. Relax and enjoy your evening; turn your cell phone back on, go see Jenny's new kittens, and know that you have gotten past the absolute hardest part of writing your applications essay.

Oh, and just one more thing: at this stage, I would be extremely hesitant to share any details of what you have already accomplished with any of your friends or parents. Even though you have gotten off to a good start — perhaps even better than you dared hoped and you are damn proud of that fact — your essay is still too fragile to be bandied about. This remains your baby to hold and nurse; no passing it off. Similar to reading those other essays at this juncture, discussing it at any length may cause unnecessary doubts to begin to seep in. So, if any well-intended questions are asked, just respond with something basic, along the lines of "Yeah, it went okay," or "Well, it still needs a lot of work," and let it go at that.

Picture a stone carver not allowing anyone to see his sculpture before it is finished, lest someone points out a flaw or makes a suggestion that will in turn upset the remainder of the work because the creative flow in his imagination has been interrupted or redirected. There will be plenty of opportunity for constructive criticism, proofreading, "tweaking," and "polishing up" once the basic essay-carving has been completed. For the nonce, this is your work and yours alone.

Chapter 12

Ready, Set, Write
(Phases II and III)

ongratulations. When last we parted, you had made a good solid start on your applications essay. With any luck you have heeded the advice not to discuss any of the particulars, or, if you did not heed that advice, you have not been distracted or deterred in any way. Bear in mind, there is a long way to go — but it will be much easier this time around because you have taken that all-important and most terrifying essay-leap of all: the start.

No matter whether you actually made it all the way through the first draft or only partly, there is an additional "side bonus" to having come this far that you may or may not be aware of: even while you were playing with the kittens or riding with Eric after that first effort, your mind was subconsciously working away. Like a cow chewing its cud, your creative subconscious loves to ruminate over what you have accomplished thus far and what you hope to accomplish at your next sitting (this one), which is completing or revising that first draft. You may or may not have actively permitted yourself to think about the task, but in truth, there was thinking being done — and plenty of it.

Let's get right into another set of suggestions that may help you at this stage of the writing, and I will first address the partially-completed essay:

When you return to work, read through what you have already written, but do not waste time getting hung up on some of those highlights or ++++++ marks from the last time. It will be far too easy to become entangled with those and thus have little energy for continuing where you left off. The more "anal" of us want to have everything *just right* before we continue (trust me; I am guilty, guilty, guilty on that charge), but this is one of those times that it is best to ignore the *make-it-just-right* compulsion and move on. I know, it is especially tempting to work out those ++++++ parts and take out the thesaurus and dictionary to break the scourge of yellow fever, but the purpose of this read-through is to get you back into the "feel" of your essay so that you can go forward with it from the point where you left off. You will no doubt also find some minor glitches, spelling, punctuation, and such, but do not waste undue time rectifying them. If it is a quick fix, such as adding or deleting a period, or a right click to fix the spelling, that is fine, but nothing more (such as looking something up) should be attempted because it might lead to unnecessary distraction and delay.

Picture, again, that stone carver. Let's say he is working on a statue of [well, you fill in the subject; it is your mental image]. On day one, he roughs out the head, torso, and arms, and then leaves for the night. Next morning, he comes in and sees all the flaws, rough spots, and whatever else bothers him about the head, torso, and arms, and rather than continuing on with the legs and feet, he begins to re-work the first part. Two things unquestionably happen: 1) he risks losing the sense of proportion to the overall statue and 2) he ends up too tired to work his way any further. Even worse, a third and fourth crises might also occur: he will no doubt raise more flaws that will have to be fixed, and — worst case scenario — he could end up ruining the original work and having to abandon the project altogether and begin anew.

I will tell you that the only thing I honestly feel that is worse than having to psyche yourself up for that first attempt at essay-writing, especially if you truly dreaded the thought, will be having to psyche yourself up for that first attempt a second time. You will be depressed, distressed, and afraid that you will fail again — too much pressure, and valuable time has passed … the perceived monster that you thought you had slain regains its original size and grows even more.

So, when you return to your essay, read it through once or twice for re-familiarization purposes and then proceed from there. Not only will this help to avoid our stone carver's fate, but you might also actually find that right word or what you meant to say in the +++++ spot as you move forward and your creative juices start to trickle again. I should also add that you will most likely be adding some more highlights and new ++++++ notations, so all your "anal" efforts to make things look neat would have gone to waste, anyway — now there are more to contend with.

Finally, as regards the partially complete effort, I urge you to do your best to finish the first draft in this sitting. This is particularly important if you have begun working on it over the weekend and do not see a chance of doing anything of significance on it for another few days. I know you are tired of hearing about my comp-instructor days, but another of the most obvious issues when reading my students' papers was a definite lack of continuity, both in thought and style. I could always tell when an assignment had been shelved too often or for too long — and how many times — simply by the changes in tone and style. (Even good, solid professional writers can have trouble maintaining this — hence the stereotype image of creative people demanding solitude and uninterrupted work time and becoming quite adamant about it.) You in reality do stand a better chance of submitting a good essay if you can keep those first-draft sessions at a minimum.

All right, so you are one of those writing fools who kept those first-draft sessions to the best of all minimums: one. I do hope that you heeded my advice to put up the essay after completion, without attempting to proofread, re-write, work on highlights, or ++++++ places, because after making such a colossal and successful effort, you truly do need to take some time away and refresh your mind. This will also be helpful at other stages of the work, but not nearly as critical as after that initial completion.

By the way, and to return for a quick second to the partial-essayists, you also would be wise to shelve the work upon completion and let your mind take a 24-hour breather before plunging back in. As is becoming rapidly obvious, this is the reason you have been urged, cajoled, and reminded to not do the p-word and to give yourself plenty of time to work on this essay. Good writing does require a cooling off between drafts ... but not so much of a break that you lose that focus and continuity.

There is another essential component to good writing: revision. Dr. Kathleen Spencer — whose academic credentials include teaching at Miami of Ohio, UCLA, the University of Nebraska, Millsaps College, Sinclair Community College, and Cincinnati State Technical and Community College — stresses revision as though it is a mantra. Along with her teaching credentials, Dr. Spencer, the author of many published papers and articles and even a textbook or two, echoes the realtor's *location, location, location* with her own *revision, revision, revision*. It is her feeling that learning to revise is even more important than learning to write (although, of course, the chicken must come before the egg, or vice-versa), and after having had her as an instructor, mentor, and friend, and also seeing the value of her principle at work with my students, I agree wholeheartedly that revision is an absolute "must."

You may recall Dr. Spencer's case study (about her three stepsons' college application letters) in Chapter 7. When I first asked her if she would kindly contribute to this book, she requested a week in which to get it finished ... not just because she recently retired from Cincinnati State and therefore is busier than ever, but because she wanted time to formulate, write, and revise before submitting the case study to me. So let this be a good example to follow: if someone as capable, accomplished, and erudite as Kathleen Spencer still feels she needs to draft and revise something as relatively simple as that case study, I do not think any of us should feel that revision is a waste of time — or take it as any indication that our writing skills lack credence.

All right, after you have finished your first draft and put it aside for a day, let's get to the first revision stage. At this juncture, I would suggest going ahead and taking care of the single-word highlights (word-choices, spellings, or whatever else you marked as such). As foretold in the previous chapter, I have a few words to say about the "spell-check" function on your computer, and now is as good a time as any to bring it up:

Do NOT rely on spell-check.

Spell-check is a valuable tool, but it is not the cure-all; at best, it is a panacea that lulls you into a false sense of security about the "correctness" of your writing. As you are well aware, the English language has many homonyms (words that sound alike, in case you [u] have been napping or the text-messaging abbreviations have overtaken control for [4] now). Along with the incredibly basic words such as "to," "two," and "too," there are more complex words that can easily be mixed up: *She road down the rode on her horse. The principle's first principal for his students was honesty. Weather it rains or snows, the whether cannot hold us up. In a vein attempt to stop the bleeding, she covered her vain.* In case you have not figured it out, those homonyms have been deliberately switched. The point is, spell-check would not have caught any of those errors; it is up to you to ensure you use the correct spelling or word-form accordingly. There are also times when spell-check just fails to recognize a misspelled word. Nothing is perfect.

Along with spell-check's little red squiggly line, there is another computer-assist aide: grammar-check, regularly denoted by a similar green line. This will help to catch some errors — mainly punctuation, or if the sentence does not make sense as written — but again, it is anything but foolproof. A classic example of a sentence that might be totally incorrect, but devoid of any red or green squiggle-lines would be something like this: *Tom said he was defiantly going to talk to his father about going to Auburn.* Did Tom intend to show "attitude" with his father (a Georgia alumnus), or was the sentence supposed to say that Tom would *definitely* talk about attending Auburn? Obviously, spell/grammar-check would give this sentence a clean bill of non-squiggled health, but unless Tom and his father are truly at odds, this is incorrect.

Bear in mind, computers are only as smart as the human being who is tickling their keyboards and reading the monitor, so take care to avoid such mistakes, especially by reason of over-reliance on these "check" functions.

So ... now that you have used your thesaurus and dictionary to clear up the highlighted words, let's tackle those ++++++ spots; the places where you thought you had something more to say, but it just did not come to you right then. As you expectantly recall, the reason I suggested using a technique such as this is that it is incredibly easy, when writing an essay, to think "Hmmm ... I know I should put something here to connect better with the next paragraph — I will come back to it later" — but trust me, your chances of totally forgetting about this are really high unless you have designated such a place. Now that you have finished the essay, chances are these "missing links" will be more easily connected because you know where your essay has ended up and it is just a matter of filling in the blanks.

In the previous chapter, when talking about the reason for ++++++, I also mentioned proofreading your work. Of course, you yourself will proof-read — and carefully — several times before this thing can be put to bed (that is journalism-speak for "is finished"), but you must, must, <u>must</u> also ask someone else to do the same. Relying on only your own proofing is about as "iffy" as relying solely on spell/grammar-check; you will catch some things, certainly, but many others will slide by. The easy explanation for this is that you just want to get the %%$$^! thing finished, and there-fore might speed up and not pay as close attention as you should; the more in-depth explanation is that your eyes (and brain's "ears") will tend to see and hear what <u>you</u> know you mean to say. Even though you know better, Tom's *defiantly* will quite frequently look/sound as *definitely* to you because that is what is intended — but to me (or another proofer), that *defiantly* and *definitely* will virtually scream *fowl* — er, I mean *foul.*

Again I defer to Dr. Spencer, who not only suggests that you have a sec-ond proofreader, but also that you try reading your essay backwards — not word-by-word, but sentence-by-sentence. This is quite awkward, and meant to be so. One of the reasons proofing our own work is so unreliable is that we have become so used to reading things left-to-right, with sen-tences that (with any luck) flow well together, that we become lazy, and our minds can wander or overlook mistakes. Think of how mindlessly we drive our vehicles; the motions and signals and such become so automatic that — as long as things are moving smoothly — we frequently give little conscious notice of the effort we are making to drive. A good way to shake that up would be to go to London, or some other place where the traf-fic runs opposite ours and we have to pay extremely close attention, or else. Likewise, and although not as potentially lethal, by forcing ourselves to read backwards, we are not lulled into a false sense of security by the smooth-flowing sentences; we must pay closer attention, and therefore er-rors will tend to catch our eye/ear more readily.

Let's move on and talk about the other part of revision, the one that encompasses more your intention and the thesis (or main idea) of your essay. This will be more easily done now that you have cleared up the technical highlights and filled in the missing gaps. To start, try to clear your mind and pretend that you are reading someone else's work. Ask yourself the following:

- Does the introductory sentence "hook" and "grab" attention?
- Does the introductory paragraph "hold" attention, and also give a good overview of the subject/thesis (mission statement)?
- Do the next paragraphs stay focused on the main idea?
- Does every sentence lead well into the next sentence?
- Does every paragraph lead well into the next paragraph? Does each paragraph complete its purpose before moving on t o the next?
- Is there a continual "flow," a stream of thought that your reader will be able to follow?
- When the essay is nearing its end, do the next-to-last few paragraphs start leading toward the conclusion?
- Is the conclusion well-stated; does it round out and offer closure to what the essay wants to say? Does it make a nice bookend to complement that other bookend — the introductory paragraph?
- Does the tone stay consistent throughout?
- Does your essay focus on the required prompt? Or if the prompt is in the form of a question, did you actually answer it?
- Have you avoided over-repetition of certain words or phrases?

This last bullet-point is a classic shortcoming with many student essays, and can be detected more readily with another of Dr. Spencer's suggestions: read the essay aloud. Yes, aloud — and to yourself at this point — but you will be amazed at how much of a difference this will make. Not only will your real ear tend to notice the audible repetition more easily than your mind's ear, but this is also where many punctuation issues will be found — especially as it applies to the comma. Read it as if you are in front of a live audience that needs to understand what you are saying.

Many of my students seemed to have trouble recalling putting the comma *before*, and not *after*, a conjunction, such as in the following [incorrect sentences]: *Jane went to the football game and, she sat with the cheerleaders. Larry tried to make the field goal but, the wind was too strong. Tom could go to Auburn or, he could go to Georgia.* What I used to try to tell them (and avoiding any technical rules of English grammar that I have long forgotten, if indeed I ever knew) was to think of a comma as the point in which they would hesitate or pause in their spoken sentences: *Jane went to the game, and she sat with the cheerleaders. Larry attempted the kick, but the wind was too strong. Tom could go to Auburn, or he could go to Georgia.* Although they would still write their essays incorrectly, when they read aloud in class, they would almost invariably catch the comma-error (and by the way, repetition as well).

- Make a quick Ctrl+F to ensure that you have not missed any ++++++ spots. Although I suggested using them to catch your eye, at this point and because you have been working so hard, they too can blend into the essay's woodwork.

- Finally, do not forget to check your dummy file (see Chapter 11) for thoughts/sentences/paragraphs you might have tucked away for future consideration. There is a good chance you will not end up using anything at all from that file — but an equal possibility that you find something for which there is now an appropriate place and you may have forgotten all about it during the course of writing.

If any of the above bullet-points need to be addressed and you can see a way to make the improvement, then do so. Though, it might serve well at this stage of the game, now that you have coaxed all this output from the inside, to seek outside input. Parents and friends are okay, but it would in all probability be more beneficial to have the help of one of your teachers (preferably English teachers as reading and correcting papers goes with the job) or guidance counselors, who may have helped you get your start on this project and are more likely (as educators) to know how this essay will hold up in front of its most important audience — the admissions committee.

You might also want feedback from several sources, and this is fine, but be wary of inviting too many proverbial cooks, and therefore risking a spoiled soup. This is entirely up to you; I leave it to your good judgment. In my opinion, though, seeking prior help from a variety of sources is far more important and helpful than inviting a whole team of post-effort critics into the mix. You have come this far, you are almost finished; let's just have one or two solid, educated critics and get this thing over with.

After having gotten the feedback — whatever amount you have solicited — it is time to work on your final revision. There is truly no way that I can sit here and make suggestions or tell you <u>exactly</u> how to final-adjust your work (after all, I have not seen it), but an excellent rule of writer's-thumb is to take all your reviewers' comments and see which ones (if any) are duplicated. If there is a particular word or phrase that all of them have questioned, chances are it needs a fix; if there is a specific place that only one of them seems to feel is tweak-able, go with your own instincts. Take note that just because someone of higher knowledge sees something one way, it does not <u>necessarily</u> mean what you said needs to be changed completely; perhaps just some minor clarification (if you choose to do anything at all) will suffice. But if something seems unclear or incorrectly stated at this stage, it is quite possible, even probable, that an admissions committee will remark on the same issue.

After all this is finished, go back over, once or twice, using the bullet-points from the past couple of pages … and then put the essay up for 24 hours and read it one more time, aloud, before making it ready for mailing.

Chapter 13

You Have Written — Now Wait and Listen

After you have received your constructive criticism from whomever you have asked for advice and proofreading, when all of your revising has been finished, either copy and paste it onto the application online for submission or, if mailing, print off that marvelous self-praising-but-humble masterpiece or and get your application packet(s) together.

I am sure that by now you are aware (or someone has gently advised you) that the essay's format should be straightforward: 12-point font in a standard style such as Times New Roman or Arial, double-spaced, and single-side of paper, complete with headers and page numbers. The title should be centered but not displayed in bold, large, or frilly font (my students used to <u>love</u> to do this); do not include pictures or clip art, and if mailing, the paper itself should be of good solid quality and laser-printed (less chance for smudging) if at all possible. All of this was most likely spelled out in the college's guide to the requirements for application; I am just reminding you. What you want to present to the admissions committee is not only a well-written and interesting essay, but one whose professional appearance bespeaks of a student with serious college aspirations.

Before you submit or send off that packet or packets, make copies of <u>everything</u> that is being sent and, of course, hold on to any electronic files of not only your application essay, but everything. Take the time, if mailing, and spend the additional cost of sending everything certified/return receipt requested; this way, you will have proof of when the packet was sent (especially in case the deadline is extremely close), and also when it was received. The post office should be able to give you a rough idea when the materials should arrive at the intended destination, and if it seems to be taking too long to hear back, a tracer can be run to ensure the package was not lost.

Also, if the college is nearby and you decide to hand-deliver your package to the admissions office, make sure you get a signed, dated/time-stamped receipt from whoever receives it. Regardless of how that packet gets to the college, you want to be certain to have proof that you have done your part to make timely application; you have worked too hard and come too far to become lazy or careless in this all-important step of actually delivering the goods.

Most applications are now done completely online, which has good and bad points. It saves printing and having the print cartridge ready, and you do not need to worry about snail mail and how long it takes to get there. But you must also realize that if your internet or their server goes down, or if you wait until the last minute to send your application online and everything is moving extremely slow (because you are not the only one to wait until the last minute) than you need to be prepared for that as well. The best way to avoid these types of disasters is to submit everything ahead of the deadline. You still need to save a copy of everything you submit on your hard drive, flash drive, and even a paper copy of it, as you never know when this may come in handy. As I stated in previous chapters; you may be able to use it all again with a few tweaks, or if you have an interview, you will need to remember what you sent in as well. There are also some variations online when submitting applications to different colleges. For most applications, once you send your essay, it is on its way and you cannot recall it for any reason. There are some colleges that may allow you to submit it for example, a total of three times, so if you make an error, they give you a chance to fix it. Do not count on this though. Make sure when you click on that submit button, that is your final essay.

Now comes that awful time of waiting, waiting, waiting. As we briefly discussed in an earlier chapter, colleges and universities do not always respond — either negatively or positively — in a short time. One of our case studies heard back within days, but this is not always the case. I have seen two to six weeks of waiting, as well as months. Some colleges have a certain date that they contact everyone, with some as late as April of your senior year. You must be patient, go about your daily affairs, and try to keep a positive outlook — with all options remaining open. You may not know exactly where you will attend, but you have at least narrowed down the possibilities, and you do know that, come August or September, the chances are real darn good that you will be a college student.

Time factor aside, you may find yourself in the position that a couple of our case studies revealed — acceptance into several institutions. While you are waiting, this might be the best opportunity to start thinking along the lines of if/then, and again keeping an optimistic frame of mind: *If Ohio*

State and Ohio University both accept me, I think I would prefer to be near a larger city, so Columbus it is … but if Ohio U accepts me, and not OSU, I did like Athens, even if it is not so big. Look at it this way: after examining all your options, every college to which you made application did appeal to you for some reason or other; therefore, regardless of which ones respond favorably, there is something to look forward to and a reason you made such a concerted effort to apply. Then there also comes the reality check; which college will finance me the best? Some schools offer huge scholarships, but when you total it all up, the amount left over that has to come out of your pocket may be more than the ones who offer little to nothing. Loans, or rather the less loans the better, should play a major role in your decision as well.

And since you have to wait anyway, I hope you will stick around now for another few pages in which you will be treated to some of "Ms. Hahn's Favorite Lectures About the Importance of Writing." When I have finished

— and I promise to try to keep it brief — I have included an additional summation-type chapter written by my co-author that will complement what I have been saying all along. Of course, as we are two different people and two different writers, there will be differences; though, the key similarity upon which we both agree is that writing the college application essay is something of extreme importance and of which you can be incredibly proud once it is finished.

In and of itself, the essay is not only your potential key to unlocking the doorway to higher education; it is also a strong reminder that you can accomplish anything you truly put your mind to — if you want it badly enough. Furthermore, the writing/technique skills you have developed up until and including this essay, either on your own or with the help of books such as this, will help you immensely and be honed to sharper ability throughout not only your college career, but throughout your life as well.

So, why all the fuss about writing? Why is so much importance placed on something that, according to many, has been allowed to disintegrate so badly over the past 40-50 years? Please allow me to share with you my most basic, bottom-line feeling about that, and the answer I always gave my students when they whined and moaned about having to write THREE WHOLE PAGES *gasp* <u>THREE WHOLE PAGES</u>?!?!?

If you truly cut everything to the proverbial chase, writing and the ability to read it is the gift that separates us humans from any of the other sentient beings with whom we share this planet. No, seriously; think about it. As I sit here on my patio writing on this warm June morning, I hear at least three different bird-species calling to and answering one another, cicadas are buzzing and crickets chirping, two of my four cats are expressing dismay at each other in a playful wrestling match-turned-ugly, and my dog Hazel is barking at the mail carrier.

I live next to the woods, and overnight, I heard deer blowing, raccoons chirring, frogs croaking, and an owl hooting. All of these creatures are communicating, in whatever way nature has equipped them, but none of them are able to record their present thoughts and feelings so that their future generations can read, ponder, and discuss — and learn from. If those deer and raccoons were able to read detailed accounts of events suffered by some of their predecessors, maybe I would not see so many of them lying dead in the road, the victims of not understanding that those man-made cars can and will crush them.

Although I admit to being the world's sorriest English major (I have absolutely no intention of reading any more Shakespeare or Chaucer than I already have had to do), I truly do marvel at the thought of those works having been written 500 or more years ago that can still be read today. Ancient Greek and Roman philosophers apparently had much time on their hands to just sit around musing life, but they left us with the essence (albeit boooorrring to read at times) on humankind discovering itself and developing as a species. Also, for the more religious among us, consider the importance and spiritual value placed on the Bible, Talmud, and Quran.

Everything we know about our history, whether as serious as wars or recreational as professional athletics, is written down for future generations to read. Any medical discoveries that will maybe help us live longer or be more productive — or the potential for unwanted side-effects — are passed along and recorded through the written word. The daily newspaper, the office memo, even your &*^^% text-messaging all reveal the importance and convenience of being able to communicate and share with each other in ways no other creature can do.

Up to this point, my students would listen respectfully enough (maybe even stop text-messaging when I brought it up), but as soon as I paused for breath would come the inevitable arguments: *But, Ms. Hahn, I am going into the Auto Mechanic/Chef/Accounting/Surveying/Criminal Justice/ Firefighter-EMT Program. What difference does it make if I learn where to put commas or just use Spell-Check instead of the dictionary? I am not going to have to write.*

Bull sh — er, cookies, and *au contraire*, my young friends. I do not want to burst your safe-from-writing bubble, but the first thing I would like to point out is that whatever your aspirations are today, the future may alter them, and you should be prepared as best and be as well-rounded as possible. I am the first to admit that I wish I could learn algebra, because that would make me a better-equipped and more complete individual, but we are not talking about me or math here. Besides, I am 50 years old and it is real well-established that writing and editing are my meal ticket; your career futures are still in an awfully malleable form.

Of the career choices I mentioned above, and I deliberately limited myself because I promised not to be too lengthy, let's first take a look at the students who are hoping for careers in law enforcement. Whether they become street cops or prison guards, the exact reason for the job, wherein they often will be confronting and dealing with hostility, may necessitate the use of force or some other means of control and/or disciplinary action. Sometimes, that use of force results in injury or death, or to a lesser importance, loss or destruction of property. And make no mistake: in this increasingly litigious society, those who aspire to a career in criminal justice — on the side of the "good guys," that is — must be prepared to write complete, solid incident reports to cover their [butts]. A crafty attorney will use anything possible, including figuratively ripping a poorly or carelessly written report to shreds — and you and/or your department may find yourself not in the witness stand, but as a defendant yourself. Did you *defiantly* read the Miranda Warning, or did you *definitely* read it? — more than a few serious felony cases have been tossed out because the suspect was not read his/her rights. (Ticky-tack, yes, but importantly so.)

And, along the lines of public service, those firefighters and ambulance people might have to explain their actions as well. Again, lives and property are at high risk when engaging in these capacities, and one must be able to report thoroughly and represent him/herself and the department well in the face of criticism and/or litigation.

Let's talk just for a moment about the other mentioned careers. Although the risk of work-related injury (to self or others) is less than that of the occupations already discussed, any time someone goes to work, there is a chance that something will go wrong and one will have to explain his or her actions. A mechanic whose hand is crushed when a car hood unexpectedly slams down, a chef who falls onto a red-hot range, a roadside surveyor who is struck by a vehicle, even an accountant who slips in a wet corridor and injures his back may have to write explanations as to the actions that led up to and caused the injury to receive compensation and/or treatment. Anyone who is on an assembly line or who works construction or mining can attest to the daily risks they face, and whenever anything goes wrong, yes, there will be oral interviews, but I can assure you there will be written reports as well — reports that will be filed and saved for future reference in case of further dispute.

But let's get away from all the negative reasons one may have to write in seemingly word-free environments. Many of my students, despite their chosen career paths, aspired to become managers, administrators, or forepersons in their jobs. Along with the increased pay level comes more responsibility, and good writing skills are often essential to prove one can handle the load. Many times, the first indication of writing skills comes in the form of the letter one must submit expressing interest in that job-opening that will result in promotion and much higher pay.

I am not trying to say that you will need to be a best-selling author; but the basics of good writing are a habit that, once learned, will stay with you — and rightly or wrongly, they can have a ripple-effect on others whose lives are intertwined and maybe even dependent on you. Two extremely brief instances that illustrate this come to mind, again courtesy of students I taught:

One woman, an older student who was going to college for the first time, had the misfortune of learning that her husband was suffering from a genetically predisposed condition that will gradually debilitate and eventually result in his death. One day, during a typical *Ms. Hahn-against-the-I-Hate-Writing-Student* discussion, she voluntarily shared with the class just how many letters and petitions she had had to write just in the last six months alone to collect disability and treatment for her spouse.

Although she was of course never <u>told</u> this, she knew that frequently her appeals or requests were granted because, despite being a factory worker, she had always had a "knack" for writing and knew her applications were complete and reflected well in her cause. She made sure to present her case in well-worded, proof-read and professionally executed documentation, and it definitely (not defiantly) worked to her advantage.

Another student, in her mid-20s, told of how, when she and her family moved to a new school district, the teacher sent her six-year-old son home with a note asking the parent (or parents) to write a page or so describing what special needs or characteristics the boy might have. For example, did he have any specific medical conditions or needs? Did he tend to request frequent restroom trips? Was there anything unusual in the way he got along with the other kids?

I cannot state this with any true authority, but I have a more-than-sneaking suspicion that besides a genuine interest in knowing how best to help this new pupil assimilate into the class, that teacher also wanted to get an idea of what sort of home the child came from. Like it or not, a parent's poorly worded or carelessly written reply will negatively reflect upon his or her child, and the teacher (albeit subconsciously) might already "peg" the child as being less intelligent or capable. Conversely, a good showing in the parental writing — bear in mind, you do not need best-seller material, just good development and execution — will cast that same child in a more favorable light, and all before he sits down and does his own writing.

So, as you can see, there are many reasons for wanting to develop good writing skills at this stage of your life, and keep them, because they will follow you and yours more than you might imagine possible. Whether you are keyboarding the college application essay or future essays, writing business reports, covering your [butt] on the job, requesting assistance from a bureaucratic entity many miles away who does not know you from Adam and has no personal interest in your situation, or writing a letter of introduction for your child, the words and the way you express yourself on paper are a good indicator of your abilities and strengths as a person — and they do reflect on others.

If you have not already been doing so, the college application essay is a wonderful place to start setting the tone and commitment you will show whenever your life requires writing skills … oh, and by the way, have I mentioned that offers of scholarship characteristically ride on a good, solid essay?

And this does not end with your undergraduate work; if you choose to go on to graduate school, there will be more applications and essays … even if you find yourself one day pursuing a doctorate, you are never out of the woods, and the competition is even more fierce, as can be attested by a contributor and mentor of mine who wishes to remain anonymous: *I once submitted an application for an American Lit. Professorship at Muskingum College in Ohio. They promptly sent me a letter back, politely, but smugly pointing out that they had received over 700 applications for the one position.*

Whoo-boy. Writing that essay would be challenging enough, but I would hate to be the board or committee responsible for reading all those app's and trying to make the best choice. (But we are not going for your PhD just yet, so relax.)

Wherever you end up, know that the process you have endured and the hoops you have jumped have brought you to this point, you have shown resilience and commitment, and the path toward college success beckons. Enjoy the experience, make the most of it, and I hope you have found this book to be of some use. Good luck!

Conclusion

As this book and others have shown, you can see that post-high school educational options that are available to you are plentiful, and if you decide to go for it and attend college, you must recognize that the application process can be a difficult hill to climb. Nevertheless, it is manageable once you determine the choices that are most important to you, based upon the criteria that you select. Therefore, narrowing your options down to a few select schools, perhaps three to five, rather than 10 or more, is an important step towards developing a strategy that will be effective for you in determining which colleges rank at the top of your personal list.

If you wade through all of your options and take this process seriously, you are likely to gain a more positive outlook regarding the college application procedure and find it not quite so overwhelming. Since there are many steps required to complete this route, including the application form and all that goes with it, the best advice that I could possibly give you at this juncture is do not be afraid of applying. Although it may seem to be a largely daunting and complex task, it is essential to gain entrance into the college experience, and believe me, it will be worthwhile in the end. As time passes and you delve into the research, despite any reservations that you have towards the process, you may find yourself embracing the experience more and more.

Since most colleges and universities now require a formal application and essay, along with an application fee, it may be difficult to identify the most appropriate subject matter for discussion within the essay itself. Normally, most college admissions criteria permit essay selection from a variety of topics, and you are left to decide which topic will best suit your writing skills and experience. While others will ask the simple (but in reality difficult) question as to why you want to go to their school and what can you bring to them, some universities leave these essays as an option to submit with the application, and others have made them a mandatory component of the application process. For those colleges and universities with a mandatory essay, it is important to describe an event or to tell a story that is specific to you and your experiences. Regardless of the requirements, if you have any writing talent whatsoever, I strongly recommend that you develop and submit an essay for consideration when the option is open. Even though it is left up to you, anytime you see the word "optional" on a college application, it is almost as they are challenging you; testing you to see how important their application process is to you. That is why I would like to strongly urge you to go ahead and do whatever is asked if possible. I once asked an admissions director if the student should send anything that was listed as optional (such as a letter of recommendation, a resume, or an essay) and her answer was a strong yes, as they wanted to see if the applicant was willing to take that extra step for acceptance into their school. This is likely to strengthen your case and your commitment to your college career, and also support your academic record.

If you are submitting applications to some of the most prominent schools in the country, such as Harvard, Yale, Stanford, or Duke, you must possess not only exemplary standardized test and academic scores, but also the writing aptitude and ability necessary to impress the admissions committee. You may possess an incredibly high GPA with strengths in math and science, but if your writing skills are weak, the admissions committees may not view you as a favorable candidate and may only consider provisional admission or put you on deferment; meaning they are waiting to see if anyone else can take your place, with higher or better qualifications. You must prove to them that you are serious and that your writing skills are comparable to the remainder of your academic record. Believe it or not, these situations do occur more often than you might imagine. You might be a 4.0 student in high school and enrolled in honors courses, but if you have coasted by in your English classes, the admissions essay will clearly demonstrate these weaknesses. It would be an unfortunate disappointment to possess excellent grades and overall ability, but poor writing skills and clearly defined weaknesses will sink you on the essay.

But there is hope: the disconnect between your overall academic prowess and writing ability should not be a factor if you work tirelessly to develop an essay for admissions that addresses your real skills and strengths as much as possible. After all, poor writing skills will only get you so far, and then the real tests begin. Your job is to improve upon those writing abilities earlier rather than later so that you will overcome any glaring weaknesses that you might possess well in advance of the admissions essay process.

You must demonstrate to the selection committee that you are serious about your college aspirations and wish to be strongly considered for admission to the college of choice. Your essay must be thoughtful, heartfelt, and honest, and it also must reflect your personal views toward the subject matter that is being addressed. College application essay requirements may vary widely from one college to the next; though, most colleges and universities tend to follow a universal pattern or a series of guidelines when developing their essay questions for prospective applicants. And as I stated previously, many times you can use the same essay for several different colleges with a few tweaks to make it a little more personable to that particular school.

You may also find that you are more than willing to discuss those ever-important options with your friends, teachers, guidance counselors, and, most importantly, your parents so that you will gain insight into what is most vital to you when choosing a college. Your efforts should not go unnoticed by admissions personnel, and with a little bit of luck, high levels of achievement, a strong academic record, and considerable community involvement thrown in for good measure, you should be in a strong position to gain entrance into the college of your choice. What happens from this point forward is entirely up to you and you alone, and you must take advantages of any opportunities as they present themselves.

I am not trying to scare you, but one way to approach the admissions essay is to view this as an exercise in strength and power, as a means of discovering what is inside you and how to grasp the meaning behind what you represent as a human being, to yourself, and to others. In this context, you know yourself better than anyone, and so you must identify those qualities and attributes that best describe you and your abilities without reservation. One of the best ways to develop your thoughts prior to writing the application essay is to improve your understanding of yourself. It is recommended that you engage in an act of self-discovery through a preliminary writing exercise. This may be accomplished in a variety of ways; though, the most feasible and simplest approach is to choose a topic, whether it is required by the admissions committee or a choice of your own, and to write down your ideas regarding the topic in a journal or type them on your computer screen. You should complete this task without the intent to write in an organized format. In other words, you should write down any thoughts and concepts as they pop into your head. They do not have to be formal sentences; rather, they could be bullet-points or other short phrases that best describe your thoughts regarding the topic of choice.

Your commitment to this exercise will shine through once you get started, and you begin to feel comfortable with writing your thoughts down on paper. You will also significantly improve your chances of writing a successful and thought-provoking essay if you develop your ideas on paper first in a less organized format. This may be viewed as a futile exercise by some, but in my opinion and from my own experiences as a writer, your focus will improve, your commitment to the project will be protected, and your confidence as a writer will grow. When you are required to write anything, even if it is a letter to a friend, you do not want to sound ridiculous or brainless, and therefore, you should always think about what you want to say before you actually write it. This exercise is no different, and, by writing an outline beforehand, you will improve your chances of writing a solid essay to impress the college admissions board.

The concept of pre-writing is always encouraged, as it enables you to put your innermost thoughts and ideas into words on paper. After writing down these, reflections, you might think that a change to your approach is necessary, but you would not have been able to make that determination if you had not engaged in this exercise. Developing your thoughts and ideas into words may seem easy to some, but this can be extremely difficult for many people. You are responsible for making sure that the words that you submit to the admissions committee in the form of an organized essay are your true opinions and feelings regarding the subject matter of choice, and

this task is often easier said than done. You can alleviate much of the stress associated with this undertaking by engaging in a pre-writing exercise. Although most of us are exceptionally busy trying to balance our personal, professional, and academic lives, writing down your thoughts and beliefs from time to time is a positive means of gathering your ideas and putting them into words that make sense to you. Writing an admissions essay is a project in and of itself, and therefore your approach should incorporate the identification of your most important thoughts and beliefs prior to developing an organized essay.

I would recommend giving yourself a window of several months prior to the college application due date to begin the process of idea generation and essay development. Take it one step at a time. You could begin by writing down your ideas and opinions a little bit at a time, perhaps a few notes every night until the time comes when they must be organized into an essay. The concepts that you generate early on may be some of your best, and so it is important to give yourself sufficient time to develop these and to determine if you are headed in the right direction with them. Your ideas are your own and what you make of them is entirely up to you, but I strongly recommend that you identify what they are and what they mean to you as soon as possible. The sooner that you can identify your thoughts and put them down on paper, the better off you are in getting the creative juices flowing and in developing an essay that is worthy of your talents and strengths. The opportunities in completing the application essay are end-less, but if you do not take the time that is necessary to accomplish these objectives, you will be sorely disappointed.

Think of it this way: It has taken you 17 to 18 years to get to this point in your life, and during this period, you have experienced many different things. How could you possibly identify your skills, evaluate your strengths, and consider your primary objectives in one evening with any sense of value or merit? This exercise would be almost impossible to accomplish. Therefore, you must start early and work on your essay a little bit at a time so that you are not stuck at the absolute end, the night before an application deadline, with a weak essay and a limited opportunity for admission. Keep the ideas flowing from the beginning, identify your talents and abilities, write them down, and see where this process takes you.

The way in which you approach this venture does not in reality matter; in other words, whether you keep a journal, word document, or piece of paper with your ideas is irrelevant; the important part is that you keep track of these concepts at all. This may seem like a difficult mission to accomplish, but you are likely to benefit significantly from this process, and it will also improve your chances of writing an admissions essay that will be strong, full of meaningful content, and reflective from the beginning.

If you are writer at heart, the essay for admission may not be so difficult to accomplish. In other words, you might find yourself in the enviable position of writing an essay that does not require a significant amount of time or energy on your part, and that also flows easily and works to your advantage in gaining favorable reviews from the admissions committee. But if you are like most of us, including me, you are likely to encounter a number of difficulties in your efforts to develop a thought-provoking and important essay from scratch. It is extremely difficult for most of us to discover that creative place in our minds that allows us to advance our thoughts and beliefs regarding a particular topic to a place that enables us to translate them onto paper or a computer screen. Many of us who are born with a scientific brain will have incredible difficulty accomplishing an undertaking of this nature, since we are not likely to tap into our imaginative sides all that often. Therefore, the pre-writing exercise may be more imperative than ever, and it also may demonstrate that you are not as weak a writer as you once believed.

Either way, a commitment to this process is important and is required for any person, even if he or she possesses a strong and skilled writing talent, since all writers must experience and then express themselves through words. Your words may look different from those written by everyone else, but the most important thing to recall is that they are yours and yours alone. For many of us, there are so few things that we can call our own.

Our words represent both the best and worst of us, and this exercise is critical in enabling ourselves to tap into something that might have been hidden since birth. Your job is to dig deep into those internal resources and engage in a period of self-discovery, since this process will lead you to a place that will facilitate success over the course of your life.

In essence, your writing abilities to this point have led you down a specific path. You may consider yourself a mediocre, average, or even an excellent writer. You may find that writing comes to you easily, or it is perhaps the most difficult mission you have yet to come across. Your job in writing the college application essay may require you to tackle what you may think to be a mountain, while for another person, this might be the tiniest molehill in the world. Regardless of your writing talents, you are likely to perform to the best of your ability when you concentrate and focus on what is most important to you. The college admissions essay may be a difficult task to accomplish, but you will gain a significant amount of satisfaction from creating a product that will improve your chances of moving on with your academic pursuits in the desired manner.

Your goals and objectives in performing this exercise are likely to be different from those of your friends, but bear in mind that your role in creating a successful essay is to identify what things are most vital to <u>you</u>. You may find value and importance in an undertaking such as community service, while your friends may value different concepts altogether.

But, let's assume for the sake of discussion you find that you are interested in community service and have volunteered during your high school years. This may be an excellent way to tap into your inner being and demonstrate to the college admissions committee that you are more than just a number, and also that you are a human being with a worthwhile set of abilities to contribute. In this community service example (and we did see a case study that addressed this scenario), your role as a college applicant is to identify how your volunteer experience or community service activities have shaped who you are today; not only how it made a difference to someone else, but also how it impacted you. This may be discovered through such characteristics as your concern for others and their plight, sensitivity towards those that are less fortunate than you, and your willingness to assist these persons. If you played a role in coming up with the idea or leading and organizing the activity also needs to be addressed. Many times, it is believed that some high school students would rather go to the mall or play sports than perform acts of community service, but for some of you, the latter may be your calling and duty. If you enjoy this kind of activity in your spare time, write about it in your admissions essay. This would serve as a topic that you place close to your heart, and it is something in which you have identified a sense of value and belonging.

You are not writing this for your friends, or they for you. Your jobs are the same, though: to produce a high-quality, engaging, and interesting essay that demonstrates the value that you bring to the table at the college or university of your choice; what you can bring to them. You are responsible for taking the time that is necessary to produce an essay that best suits your talents and strengths, while masking your weaknesses as best as you can.

From a purely creative standpoint, writing the college application essay requires you to take the time to learn about yourself and the type of contribution you can, and with any bit of luck, will provide to your environment. The admissions essay is a requirement that is mandated by most colleges and universities in order for their respective committees to get to know you better and to assess your writing and creative abilities. This essay for admission also serves a second purpose: to allow you as a maturing student to understand what makes you tick and what enables you to be creative, and also insightful, and finally, what makes you the person that you are today. This serves as the foundation toward improving your life and dedication to the people and things you love and value most. If you do not take the time to get to know yourself properly, you may be able to coast through life for a long time, but you will never truly accomplish anything of value.

In truth, the college admissions essay process should serve a dual role. You need to get to know yourself to grow, and this is only accomplished through a period of self-reflection and evaluation, during which you might improve yourself and the contribution that you bring to your life and those who surround you. I have recently discovered that many of my values have changed over time and that the things that I used to place genuine importance in are now less meaningful, while my friends, family, and personal aspirations have become the most important things in my life. Unfortunately, I learned these lessons in my late 20s and early 30s, but I hope that you begin to discover those things now while you are still in high school. They will provide a significant amount of benefit to you at an early, yet highly impressionable, age, and you are likely to carry them throughout your college experiences and beyond. I recommend that you use the college application essay as a source of self-reflection and discovery so that you will possess the talents and attributes that will enable you to succeed in whichever college experience you choose.

You must embrace your goals to achieve your destiny, and with perseverance and a positive attitude, you will succeed. College is an excellent place to begin.

Appendix 1

Self-Reflection and Application Essay(s)

© 2004 Kathy L. Hahn

As mentioned in the Introduction, the following pages are a good example not only of self-reflection, but of how a seemingly non-conforming application essay might be accepted. Originally written for a core Theology course, upon suggestion from my professor, I took a chance and included it in my application packet for grad school. At first pass, one might wonder how a Jesuit institution would view this … but bear in mind that despite what it may initially seem, I and many of the Jesuit spiritual concepts agree (if one takes the time to truly read into the essays) that I gave a fair and honest representation of myself, what I had already achieved, and what I further hoped to achieve. I also wish to reiterate that these are my words, thoughts, and opinions — mine and mine alone.

Essays

Before I begin, I need to state that I am almost 47 years old, and at this age, I feel entitled to employ some degree of "Life Experience" license — similar to the concept of "poetic license" — when answering the questions. Because I started college at a later stage in life, these essays-turned-application essay are my first attempt at doing such, and I look forward to hearing your response.

Thinking About Ritual

Religion, as I would define it, is one's way of acknowledging that perhaps there is some Power greater than oneself and having faith that said Power will always be there as a means of guidance, support, and comfort. My admittedly simple definition includes components of faith but strongly lacks any certainty or conviction as to just how that Power came into being, what it has in store for us, or the rewards/punishments for, respectively, belief and non-belief. At various times almost all of us seek the already mentioned guidance, support, and comfort. By appealing to something superhuman for such spiritual amenities, one can always hope that no matter what the outcome of one's prayers, appeals, or questions, that the higher Power always knows what is best, and that there are good reasons well beyond one's ken to explain why things sometimes do not go as planned or hoped. Religion, therefore, is to some extent an omnipresent placebo-a 24/7 operator standing by for consultation and, simultaneously, a "cure-all" remedy to explain all that which we mortal human beings find difficult to understand or accept.

Furthermore, religion instills a certain amount of discipline, oftentimes including rituals and certain customs, which one may either hold on to as one goes through life or abandon in favor of something that seems better suited. While I am not as familiar with various religions as I could be, some immediate examples that come to mind are the Catholic ritual of praying the rosary, the Islam custom of stopping to pray five times daily, and the Jewish Passover service. While some members of various faiths hold on to, cherish, and pass along such rituals, perhaps over time the repetitions can lose their meaning; their effectiveness as a channel to whatever Power wanes or is no longer valid. In that case, a disenchanted faction of a group, or a single individual, must decide if a simple modification of ritual will suffice, or if an entire overhaul and possible change to another faith are necessary.

Raised as a Protestant, my own personal childhood experiences in the Church of Christ led me to a very early exodus (no pun intended) to any sort of "organized" religion. I was quite young when it occurred to me that I actually felt closer to what I believe is the concept of God when I was anywhere BUT at the Sunday School church services I was made to attend! I also somehow understood that just because I showed up at a certain place and time on Sundays, and once there could recite Bible verses, offer an extemporaneous group prayer if called upon, or learn all the words to a hymn-those things did not necessarily make me a "good Christian."

But I was encouraged to perform, to display my memorization abilities, all too often. The mere repetition and routine recitation of such stock words and phrases, delivered as ritual, very quickly lost any meaning they might once have had for me, or any impression they made on me. They did, actually, sound superficial, shallow, and insipid — not that I could have voiced it as such back then. And although I already had a relatively strong vocabulary, I probably did not know the meaning of a full one-third of the Bible-verse words I was made to memorize — but hey, that did not matter; so long as I parroted on command, I received the symbolic crackers of praise.

Another, more telling ritual in my Protestant upbringing was the notion of baptism, and I rejected that as well ... not because I could not find comfort in the idea of salvation; rather, the whole "ceremony" about it struck me as being phony — almost a circus act, or magic trick, performed more for the entertainment of the crowd and/or the evangelical emcee than the one to be saved. Accordingly, when I stated my desire to be baptized privately, as opposed to in front of a group of people, I was told that this HAD to be done in public; I should be *proud* to have everyone watching me accept Jesus Christ as my Savior. But when I voiced my opinion that so long as God saw (after all, He was the only audience of any substantial meaning), I might as well have spoken heresy. Needless to say, I rebelled and was not baptized then.

Before I leave the subject of that ritual, I should note that everyone expressing concern for my salvation took heart in the fact that I had been christened/baptized at six months, and therefore was probably safe. But, this made no sense whatsoever to me; I wanted to shout: *C'mon, wait a minute, people! Time out! What you all are telling me is that something that was done when I was too young to know any different, too helpless to make my own choice, and too small and weak to resist even if I wanted to — you're telling me that THAT ritual will have more standing in the eyes of God than something I as an independent, young adult have made a conscious decision to do? — but would prefer to do privately, unlike when I was apparently dangled by the heels and dipped in, or sprinkled with a dollop from a fount of patriarchal hypocrisy disguised as salvation?*

I was once kicked out of Sunday School because I asked an innocent question ... the teacher flatly stated that "Anybody who does not know Jesus cannot go to heaven," and I was puzzled. Just a few nights ago, on some TV National Geographic-type special, the show concerned a recently discovered in the deepest jungles of South America an aboriginal tribe that was quite primitive. In sincere concern, and not in the least way meaning to be smart-ass, I raised my hand and asked if this meant those poor people would go to Hell just because they did not know Jesus — it did not seem fair, especially since God was supposed to be so all-forgiving. Out to the hallway with me — and I should be thinking about what I said and repenting while I stood out there for the remainder of that class.

The Church of Christ, at least back in those days, was not ready for a logical little girl with a strong sense of independence and "self," but that's fine; I endured and matured in spite of it. The ritual Sunday morning trappings became so confining that as soon as I was old enough to make my own choice, I never set foot in a formal service again. As I grew older, I found (and still find) myself taking my "God" time in the woods, or in the still of night — alone. I have been to churches only long enough to admire artwork or (as in the case of Salt Lake City) to hear a world-renowned choir rehearse. There is no set ritual to my way of interpreting God; either I am too logical or just plain independent to want to latch on to some sort of prescribed routine. However, I do offer more than one might consider my share of non-rehearsed prayers, offered both in supplication and gratification as needed; without meaning to sound cynical, I feel God is far more likely to listen to the occasional genuine, heartfelt prayer than a monotonous litany of impersonal, stock memorizations, bead-rubbings or prayer-rug unfoldings.

And, as a postscript, while I normally eschew ritual of any sort, I was formally and voluntarily baptized — at age 32 — with a sprinkle of Montana spring water and only the presiding minister, my dog, and God to witness. Somehow, I think that's how it was really meant to be, at least for me. Sincere spirituality, not ritualized formal religion with all its hang-ups, has guided me throughout my life.

Thinking About Moral Obligations

Many of my once-stated and firmly-held goals have fallen by the wayside of either impossibility or cynicism — or occasionally have been involved in fatal accidents at the unregulated and highly dangerous intersection of both. Although I do consider myself a person of high moral character, I am having difficulty forming a "list" of morals and values; hopefully, they shall reveal themselves in this entry, their importance shown in the order I address them.

First and foremost, I have always tried to live as honestly as possible, faithful to myself even in the face of adversity, and remain true and genuine despite the occasional pressures and possible rewards of doing otherwise. The best and most personal example of this is I do not hide my lesbianism, and although it has at times caused conflict (from sources as close as a non-understanding mother to those as distant as homophobic potential employers), I have never pretended heterosexuality.

There is a two-fold reason to this: No. 1, as I stated, I believe in being true to myself, and No. 2, I do not wish to misrepresent myself and possibly cause upheaval down the road for anyone else. There are too many women (particularly in my age bracket) who in their youth bowed to societal pressures and feigned heterosexuality, only to cause individual and familial chaos when they finally admitted to themselves that the husband-track really was not what they had wanted all along. Luckily, I did not fall into that societal-expectation trap, because I would not have wanted to cause such hurt or betrayal to the other human beings deeply involved with me — and really, everyone involved in this hypothetical but real-life scenario is there only because the woman betrayed herself in the first place, which I did not do.

Before I move on to another, less personal topic, I should note that I consider myself very fortunate in that somewhere, along with whatever gene-code manipulator punched in *lesbian*, that manipulator saw fit to include a few extra molecules of courage and basic indifference to the often-hostile behaviors of others toward me. So long as I am being true to myself, I can withstand any disapproval. I do not change or regulate my activities in any way that bespeak otherwise of myself, although simultaneously I proudly admit that I do not seek activities in order to militantly and radically pronounce my sexuality. This, ironically, has led me to many a fall-out with lesbian compatriots who deem my unobtrusive behavior as "denial of the cause" — but here again, I do not change my philosophies or behaviors just to impress them!

As evidenced by the rather lengthy discourse above, another moral/value issue for which I consistently striven is not to be hypocritical. While I realize it is not always considered "good," I am by nature a very judgmental person, and therefore try to live up to the judgments I make upon others. I am my own harshest critic, and if/when I myself fail to live up to the expectations I have of others, I feel I have let myself (and them) down considerably. However, inasmuch as I can be very judgmental, I am also a wonderful friend and always do my best to live up to the bargain into which one enters when offering friendship. I believe in treating people the way I wish to be treated, and if they somehow cause offense, I do try to communicate with them and talk things out before just discarding the friendship altogether. I am by nature very intimate with good friends — I withhold very little, if anything — and believe it is almost a sacred moral duty to respect the trust and try to do one's best to solidify and maintain that friendship.

Still less personal, but also a life-long belief, is to promise that any animal I bring into my home (and believe me, there have been a slew of them in my lifetime!) is fed, watered, sheltered, and — most importantly — loved. When one brings a helpless creature into one's home, one is accepting the responsibility and moral obligation to ensure that creature's well-being to the best of one's ability. Last year, when I got my current dog, Hazel, from the SPCA, I knew that once again there would be additional cost, and my freedom somewhat restricted, but these were prices I was willing to pay because I could see the dog had been mistreated (if not totally abused) and that she had no idea why she was in that cage. I abhor humans who mistreat/abuse animals, and I guess in some small way feel an occasional moral responsibility to try to make up for someone else's malfeasance along those lines. All Hazel wanted was a home and a person to treat her kindly; I knew it was within my means and values to do so. And, as dogs are wont to do, she has responded with the unconditional love that no human (including myself) can ever offer.

Speaking of homes, another goal I have achieved and hope to maintain is that I have always taken older or vacant homes and fixed them up. "Restored" is not the word, for true restoration requires financial resources beyond my own, but I have always left a place in much better shape than when I moved in. While admittedly this is a gross personalization, I feel that older homes have loved and sheltered so many human souls that they deserve to have dignity and respect accorded their own souls. I also believe we have destroyed enough of this planet, bulldozing the environment in order to erect more houses, when there are plenty available that simply need to be cared for once again.

Now, in order to take care of my all-important pets and home, I have begun a late-stage drive toward furthering my education so that I can better afford the upkeep and maintenance for both to which I feel obligated. When I embarked on this scholastic journey, I promised myself that I would apply myself diligently and to the best of my ability, and thus far have done so.

I owe this not only to myself and to those who depend on me, but also to the various grantors and scholarship awarders who have seen fit to help out economically. I have contributed a lot of my long-held financial reserves in order to facilitate this particular goal, and have deprived myself of many other ways in which that money could have been used.

Finally, as regards this section, I feel a further obligation to those advisors, professors, and instructors who have so encouraged me and taken the time to maybe offer just a wee tad more interest than usual because they do sense my sincerity and determination. I try to repay their help and interest with respect and courtesy, both in and out of the classroom, and am always willing to help other students if at all possible — great training for one of my eventual career-goals of teaching English composition!

On to the other question in this section: Of course I am unhappy if I fail to meet my goals (isn't everyone?), and to that extent, I seldom choose activities that may keep me from success. For instance, although I was never much of a party animal, it is far easier for me at age 46 to devote my entire weekend (if necessary) to studying rather than, say, going somewhere. Having lived to this age, I have developed what I feel is a great sense of priority and am pretty hard to derail once I am on track. Also, despite my having used the word "obligation" several times in this paper, I do not tend to take on any obligations that I am not willing to fulfill. Again, I think this is an age/wisdom thing, and can illustrate it with a few simple examples:

When I was younger, I felt it an obligation — regardless of the circumstances — to answer my telephone or doorbell. Now I do not; granted, as to the former it is easier now with Caller ID and such, but even without that convenience, I often ignore the ring altogether if it will interfere with something more important to me. These days, distraction equals deterrence, and for the most part I have the freedom to ignore them and continue on with my own agenda. (I have learned that the world will likewise continue on ITS own agenda without my diligence along those lines.)

I also no longer feel obligated to respond positively to an invitation. If the event is something I do not wish to attend, or if I have other matters to demand my time and attention (such as schoolwork), I simply say "Thanks" and politely decline the invitation. I am not obliged to contribute to charity (unless I want to), I do not worry if someone can tell I do not have on a bra under my sweatshirt, and I do not need to be polite to telemarketers, because they are intruding upon my privacy. (Which I would never intentionally do to them.)

Some of these examples are fairly rudimentary, some humorous; one might not actually assign any deep "moral" dilemma to them, and in fact might find them superfluous. But they are representative of the general way in which I go about my life. I answer to my own needs, hopefully do not hurt too many others along the way, and focus in on making my own life as successful and rewarding as possible within my self-determined moral and ethical boundaries. Ultimately, my own reflection is the one staring back from the mirror, and so long as I can say *You tried your best* while looking myself directly in the eye, I feel morally content with myself.

Thinking About Ethnicity and Religion

After considering the questions posed, I know that there is a good chance this part of the essay may be considered somewhat frivolous; before I begin, I assure my reader(s) that a lot of thought went into something from which there really isn't a whole lot of material to draw. Still, some of the memories evoked are quite pleasant, and they help take the superficial sting I still feel when reliving my childhood ordeals with all things religious. Truthfully, religion has never played a major role in my life — neither while I was growing up nor (certainly) not now.

Being of Protestant German/Irish heritage, I was raised with a certain acknowledgement of the beliefs once held by my ancestors; however, what little exposure I had was far more reflective only of my mother's side of the family, since my father's native German parents had passed away before I was born. My maternal grandfather was Irish, and my grandmother German, so my ethnicity finds representation even in only the maternal side. All of my family were good, conscientious citizens, and for lack of a better phrase, they could be called "God-fearing." There was a very strong work ethic handed down through the generations which is obviously inherent in me, and I of course faithfully adhere to (most of) the moral principles and values with which I was raised. But to what extent has religion, of ethnic or other origins, played in my genealogical background? — little, if any at all.

To be truthful, unless a family is really "into" religion, I think it is difficult to maintain customs and traditions, particularly those dealing with something as personal as religious faith, throughout the generations. For example, my own background is certainly not composed of atheists or even agnostics; there was always at least a nodding acquaintance to the notion of a Christian God and his son Jesus, but beyond that, it is easy to see that each generation, after having had the seeds sown and kinda-watered and semi-tended throughout childhood, pretty much left of its own accord.

The one thing that did seem to remain constant — and in keeping with the working-class, blue collar immigrant neighborhood of Northside (where both sides of the family "settled" upon arriving here) — was that the churches everyone attended were within easy walking distance and a viable part of the community. Beyond that, there does not seem to be a whole lot of religious "tradition," at least not as I interpret the questions this essay addresses. Actually, the only "tradition" I can seem to find as I retrace my memories is that nobody ever seemed to want to continue with what they were shown during youth.

For instance, I still have the small pocket-sized New Testament that Mom received upon her baptism at age 12, from the now-defunct Chase Avenue Church of Christ, which had been in Northside (corner of Chase and Brookside) for several generations. Perhaps in keeping with some sort of tradition, I was made (intentional word usage) to attend Sunday school there throughout my childhood — until that church moved to North College Hill and became the Clovernook Christian Church. Something tacitly sacred in my family's history was broken at that point, although I doubt things would have gone much differently for me, even had that church stayed on Chase Avenue; once given my own choice in the matter, I could not break away fast enough.

The main reason I mention that old pocket Bible and that particular church is that obviously my mother had also been sent (willingly or not) to Sunday classes and/or church there, and never in my entire life — until she died in 1986 — did I ever see my mother in church or Sunday school again, save perhaps for a few Easter Sundays. — Yes, up until I was about seven or so, once a year my mother dressed up of a Sunday morning and made a cameo appearance in the House of the Lord (usually the erstwhile Hoffner Street Church in Northside, which was a landmark until 1997 when a microburst toppled its mighty steeple and left the whole building unstable; the church has since been torn down and its property part of a BP convenience store ... so much for tradition.) Anyway, the point I am making is that my mother was exposed to Christian teachings — as had been her mother before her — but neither of them practiced any sort of religious ritual once they reached adulthood. Well, on second thought ...

While my mother seldom mentioned anything at all related to religion (save the occasional use of the word "goddamn"), it is only fair to report that my grandmother made frequent dutiful and more appropriate reference to God. Boy howdy, she really enjoyed watching those Bible-thumper televangelists and listening to her LP hymns on the stereo (or hi-fi, back in those halcyon days). But all this was of course quite easy from the comfort of her reclining armchair, wearing housedress or sleeping robe, with her coffee and the telephone nearby, right? And hey, if she did not like the sermon, she could always change channels! Gram also gave quite regularly to these televultures, and once sent Oral Roberts an extra five dollars when I had been constipated for about two weeks and the doctors were considering surgery ... hallelujah, my bowels finally moved, and to her dying day I think Grandma credited Reverend R. with having saved my bowels, if not my soul. (That would have taken her whole pension check, deducted at regular monthly intervals!)

Now, since with some degree of sarcasm and/or humor I've mentioned my dear grandmother, and to perhaps restore the true reverence I hold for her: About the only thing palatable to me about having to attend Sunday school in my childhood was the fact that — before my mother divorced and we to Northside ourselves — I would get to spend Saturday nights at Gram's and then on Sunday morning she would walk the mile-or-so-plus to Chase Avenue Church of Christ with me. Mind you, she never ATTENDED (recollect, she had already gotten her TV "God-fix" and dropped off the weekly stamped money envelope in her mailbox), but she did walk me most of the way there before boarding a bus to go downtown for breakfast. This became about as close to a "ritual" as I can claim along the lines of religion.

In truth, I genuinely loved those walks, and in the rose-colored lenses of my quasi-20/20 memory's eye, Sundays were always bright and warm, gently breezing, the air exhilaratingly fresh, and the feeling of being alive always spirited and joyful ... until, of course, I got to the church. Then all the proverbial wind went out of my sails, the day became figuratively cloudy, and I barely endured the (24-hour) hour-and-a-half of what I then defined as nonsense and now recognize as just that (nonsense) with an unhealthy dose of hypocrisy thrown in for good measure.

A good case in point, or nonsense? Again, Grandma plays a part:

For Christmas 1965, she and Grandpa gave me my own Bible, a white-covered, King James Red-Letter Edition (which I still have to this day, and cherish even if I seldom consult it). I would have loved to carry this Bible with me every Sunday, and have it gradually accrue that well-worn, comfy look that accompanies many beloved Bibles, BUT because I had had perfect attendance (hell, what choice did I have?) I was awarded a red-bound King James Red-Letter Edition Bible, the same exact edition save for the cover's color, and told that was THE only one I could use henceforth in class! I still have that one, too; both sit in compatible truce side-by-side on a bookshelf, their erstwhile enmity long diffused by my recognition that my own internal faith has never wavered in the face of such adversarial organized nonsensical bullshit.

And what of the aforementioned hypocrisy? Many, many instances, but I'll stick to the current one: Telling me to love and respect my elders, and simultaneously saying Leave the white Bible (so lovingly inscribed by Grandma in now-faded red ink) at home because she should not have gotten it for me, knowing I was going to win the attendance award! Jeez, shame on you, Grandma! Cannot use your Bible — the Sunday school teacher says so! (I still bristle, even as I write.)

Yes, lovely walks with Grandma aside, I hated/abhorred/detested/dreaded Sunday school. Looking back, while at the time my vocabulary and thought processes could not have adequately described this, I think I basically resented that it was Sunday — one of only two days off from school, and having to wear a damn dress, to boot — but what I most resented that while I was being force-fed a weekly helping of illogical horsecrap, my mother was in bed sleeping, my father was playing golf, Grandma was going downtown for breakfast ... even my younger brother did not always have to go because Mom did not want to have to wake up early and get him properly dressed! Hell, if church/Sunday school was so all-fired important, why in the world did not THEY have to go?!?!

Forgive me; I still quiver with indignation, and am prickling anew as I write these words. I know that my parents meant well, as did their parents, and those before, etc. — but I think they too must have realized, at some level, that religion and the notion of God cannot be enforced merely by following traditions and customs; such feelings must be decided for oneself and it is all right, after all, to decide one's own course.

So maybe, in a bemusing, ironic sort of way, I have carried on the family torch, in that as soon as I was old enough to make my own choices, I abandoned all that organized nonsense and set about discovering my own spiritual faith and the means by which to observe it. And, even if I were to try to maintain any sort of ethnic/religious traditional observances, rituals or customs, they will die with me; my elders have all passed away and I myself have never wanted children. However, I do believe I would have broken even the tradition of breaking tradition had I borne children of my own; recalling my own distress so well, I never would have forced them into going to church or Sunday School — unless I went as well, OR if they expressed an interest/desire of their own. Therefore, they would have had no "tradition" to break, even before they grew minds of their own!

Thinking About Reconciliation

Over the course of my life, there have been many times I felt "at peace" with myself, "in harmony" with my environment, and "in kinship" with others — a total reconciliation with Life and an intense desire to live it. Strangely enough, sometimes reconciliation has come in the form of completely negating a prior such sense of peace and harmony.

The best example of this? In 1988, I had the opportunity to move to Montana and live in breathtaking, mountain-surrounded pine forest solitude. I was so weary of Cincinnati (my hometown), and after the death of my mother in 1986, this whole area held nothing but painful memories for me. Furthermore, I was tired of the noise and confusion and summertime heat and humidity; I desperately longed for a major change. My then-partner and I had always craved the chance to live near abundant wildlife and experience "real" winter, and when a seemingly good job opportunity came for her, we felt it would be remiss to pass up a situation for which we had so often expressed a mutual desire.

Such a big move was of course difficult to effect, but we succeeded; once in Montana, we lived together in two great log homes over the course of five years, during which time our 17-year relationship came to a slow and painful end. Despite the personal issues, both of us truly loved the surroundings, and after we separated I lived for seven more years alone in two different Montana houses, both of which I fixed up and experienced a great deal of satisfaction from doing.

Those seven solitary years were for the most part wonderful; I immersed myself in self-education of things both practical (such as wiring a house addition) and intellectual (literature and educational television). A very typical moment of serenity and harmony would best be illustrated on an early December day amidst a steady snowfall, with the well-stocked (self-felled, cut and split) firewood pile feeding the softly crackling woodstove … my best-ever dog Sophie lying at my feet, cat Tigger on my lap, and the aroma of fresh-brewed coffee wafting throughout the house. I kept in touch with long-distance friends via email, instant messaging, and telephone, and of course forged new acquaintances (albeit not many) everywhere I lived.

The times when electricity failed were all the more gratifying because I was well-prepared with oil lamps, flashlights, and a manual can opener; the loss of television and computer was a minor price to pay for the reward of knowing I could survive — and quite well — without them. I cooked food and heated water (brought inside as fresh-fallen snow and tasting remarkably pure) on the woodstove, and put all perishables in bear-proof containers outside in the sub-freezing air. The longest such duration of power failure I ever experienced was one full week; during that period even the phone was dead because the Blackfoot Telephone generators lost their own power after two days without being fed from the electric company's downed lines. When on the eighth or ninth day the lights suddenly flickered to life, I was actually keenly disappointed; there had been absolutely no intrusion in my life, and nothing had been expected of me, for what I now believe is the most peaceful interlude I'll ever have in my life.

But the peace and serenity I had found upon reaching and embracing the mountains gradually began to lessen. I found myself pining (no pun intended) for the city, my long-time friends, and what few members of my family remained with whom I still had any semblance of a relationship. While I never lost my love of the "real" winters, I also started intensely disliking the ultra-dry western summers and continual fire threat. One always hears about and shudders at the thought of Montana winters; trust me when I tell you the summers are equally brutal, in their own way. From the end of June until mid-October or so, moisture is so scarce that one is afraid to snap one's fingers for fear the resulting friction will ignite tinder-dry needles and dead pines. The heat is relentless; the only saving grace is that, unlike in the Midwest, the nights usually do cool down once the sun dips behind the mountains. But the sun comes back up pretty early, and with it the heat; wells run dry, tempers run short and flare dangerously, and road dust pervades in continual choking clouds long after a vehicle has passed.

So, with that in mind, suddenly the Cincinnati summer humidity did not seem so repulsive, and the once-welcome solitude became overwhelming. I returned here twice in the summer of 2000 — just "testing the waters," so to speak, and in October moved back. I bought a modest home on one of the busiest streets in this city, and found the traffic noise as soothing as once had been the mountain silence. After a few long years of near-total isolation, it was wonderful to again have easy access to social and cultural amenities, and of course it was great renewing old acquaintances and bringing each other up-to-date in person instead of via email and/or telephone.

Even the memories of my mother (and now also my grandmother, who passed away while I was in Montana) no longer threatened or dismayed me. Although I still suffered her/their loss tremendously, I now felt a certain sense of peace and acceptance that the passage of time had somehow ushered in. I felt I had truly followed my heart, and that my reconciliation was now complete, in that I had come full circle and proven myself capable of a more rugged lifestyle. And because I had given myself such an extensive time-out from all the city things that had once annoyed me — including its residents — I was able to return with a fresh perspective and outlook, which included a deeper love and appreciation for others. But to be truthful, I have always been quite independent and introspective, so in all honesty — and with no shame or remorse — my own harmony and serenity have always come from within and pretty much reflect back only upon myself. So, my "deeper love and appreciation" of others are really just residual side effects; the people in my life are collateral beneficiaries, to coin an appropriate new term. I was of course happy to see loved ones — and they were happy to see me — but upon returning home, my true harmony came from within, period.

In conclusion, the example described above is just one of many times I have found a sense of peace, harmony, and reconciliation in my life, and in that statement alone lies the whole paradox of such terminology. The fact that such times have come upon me once and again shows, simply, that such feelings of total well-being are temporary and fleeting; therefore one can seize and appreciate them whenever possible but should never expect them to last. Nor should one be surprised to find that the polar opposite/reversal of one reconciliatory act might prove reconciliatory in its own time. In my opinion, traditional approaches, which might indicate a "planned" agenda, are futile, because one can never truly know from whence the next such feeling may be derived or achieved. To illustrate this by again referring to the Montana/Cincinnati story: had anyone told me in June of 1988, as I stood atop magnificent Logan Pass in Glacier National Park on a beautiful sunny day that I would experience just such a sense of total reconciliation by returning to Cincy and buying a rundown bungalow on bustling, cacophonous Colerain Avenue in the October fog of leftover summer humidity and shimmering auto exhaust, my echoing laughter from back then would still be chasing itself around the northwest Rockies!

Thinking With Silence

Saint Anthony's youthful and energetic emergence after a 20-year period of solitary reflection is a testimony to the benefit of occasionally taking a time-out to look within oneself in order to seek spiritual answers and comfort. While a full score of years away from society is unusually extensive, if that was the duration needed by Anthony to find self-reconciliation, he should not be looked upon skeptically or derisively. Self-reconciliation, in my opinion, is the main ingredient needed in order to reconcile with others; unless/until one can find internal peace, it is highly unlikely — if not impossible — to find that peace from any external source. After all, the only person with whom one shares every waking and sleeping moment of one's life — from birth to death — is oneself; without a basic harmonic accord at that crucial starting point, all further endeavors at reconciliation with the world, and others in it, are certain to fail.

In the previous essay, I alluded to the twelve years I spent living in several northwest Montana homes. To refresh the reader's memory, I had a partner for the first five years there, but when that relationship dissolved, I was for the most part totally on my own, and in retrospect I feel it is completely accurate to say a good 90 percent of the hours in those last seven years were spent in total isolation, with only myself to consult/seek reconciliation. I pondered many things, sought answers during long walks or mountain bike rides on old logging roads through the forests, and by the time I decided it was time to move back to Cincinnati, I had found a reconciliation with all that had led me to leave in the first place.

This city still hurts; scar tissue can still be penetrated when least expected, and the wounds opened afresh. Memories of my mother and grandmother (who passed away in '92 while I was in Montana) are everywhere, and I still catch myself tearing up at times when I pass a place with some long-buried memory, or a certain scent might fill the air, but it is now all right; the wounds close more quickly and with less residual pain from the healing. I no longer harbor feelings of anger or betrayal at my hometown, and new "bad feelings" have not pervaded as yet. For instance, although I have learned my ex also moved back to this area (right around the same time I did, unbeknownst to me), I have no desire to contact her or try to resurrect something that died long ago. I drive past homes I lived in and owned with her, and save for an occasional wistful mini-sigh, am content to let that part of my past remain right where it is. There is in fact a large box of I guess some forgotten belongings which she sent to me after ten years of separation, and although I do not quite have the heart to throw out the box, neither do I care to open it ... why risk a Pandoran reaction when there obviously is nothing contained therein that I have missed over the last decade? Again, as I cited in an earlier essay, with age comes wisdom; I see no reason to reopen a wound that has actually healed, and darn well.

All that aside, I know my period of near-solitude allowed me to find (from somewhere deep within myself) the mettle to accept this life-despite its bittersweet memories — and appreciate it for what it and I have to offer each other. And while many people shake their heads when they hear of how isolated I was in the mountains, anyone who has known me since childhood would not be surprised. For as long as I can remember, I have always taken refuge in self-reflection — whether in the solitary comfort of my room (or nowadays my house) or out alone in the woods. Sometimes at home I play music, but more often than not find true reflection within the comforting sounds of silence or nature's heartbeat. Long ago, I stopped making excuses to other people for my unusually strong propensity for desiring only my own company, and my newer acquaintances are beginning to respect that quality, and even seek their own a little more now that they see how comforting self-reflection can be.

In conclusion, having spent so much time in my own company, I can tell you I pretty much like myself and do find myself pretty damn trustworthy. There is always room for improvement, no question, but for the most part when I turn off the lights at night I do so with the contented feeling that comes from having done my best that day or if need be, I promise to schedule some self-time as soon as possible to work through the occasional discontent.

Appendix 2

Scholarship Websites

*P*lease Note: The following websites are by no means all-inclusive; though, I have tried to generate a good sampling so you can get the idea of a few of the various types and specific areas such offers address. As you will find, many of the websites are only the site on the whole of a list formulated within that main site.

Common

www.scholarships.com

www.fastweb.com

www.fedmoney.org/grants/p-0-scholarships.htm

www.scholarshipexperts.com/?sourceid=ct_southernst>
http://www.scholarshipexperts.com/?sourceid=ct_southernst%20

www.finaid.org/scholarships

http://scholarshipamerica.org

www.scholarshiphelp.org

http://superiorscholarship.org

www.syf.org/syf.aspx?pgID=410

www.collegescholarships.com

www.bigfuture.collegeboard.com

www.scholarshippoints.com

www.collegescholarships.com/scholarships_regional.html

www.drew.edu/depts/finaid/outsidescholarships.aspx

www.worldwidelearn.com/financial-aid/grants-scholarships.htm

Minority

www.teartaylor.com/scholarships.htm

http://staff.bcc.edu/msu/Scholarships.htm

http://scholarships.fatomei.com/minorities.html

www.finaid.org/otheraid/minority.phtml

www.aicpa.org/members/div/career/mini/smas.htm

www.archfoundation.org/aaf/aaf/Programs.Fellowships.htm

www.financialaidofficer.com/scholarship_search/minority_
scholarship.shtml

www.cse.emory.edu/sciencenet/undergrad/scholarships.html

www.brownandcaldwell.com/Scholarship_Opportunities.
asp?SVC=SO

www.collegescholarships.org/our-scholarships/minority.htm

www.jackierobinson.org/apply/index.php

Special Groups / Areas Of Interest

www.mcsf.com/site/c.ivKVLaMTIuG/b.1677655 (Children of USMC)

www.scholarships.com/art-scholarships.aspx (Creative Arts)

www.finaid.org/scholarships/prestigious.phtml (Humanities)

www.nursingscholarship.us (Nursing)

www.college-scholarships.com/christian_colleges.htm
(Religion/Christian)

http://college-financial-aid.suite101.com/article.cfm/scholarships_for_jewish_students (Religion/Judaism)

www.collegescholarships.org/scholarships/muslim-students.htm
(Religion/Muslim)

www.nsf.gov/funding/pgm_summ.jsp?pims_id=5257
(Science/Technology)

www.collegesportsscholarships.com (Sports/Athletics)

http://texashealthcareers.org/AWS_social_sciences.htm
(Social Sciences)

www.technosciencesupersite.org/scholarships.html (Technical)

www.donnareed.org/html/templates/dr_section.php?dr_section=scholar (Theater and Performing Arts)

www.afrotc.com (USAF ROTC)

You will also want to check into the scholarships and/or grants offered from within by individual institutions. There is plenty of help out there, both from these common and internal sources; if you take some time and effort, you might be surprised to find there is financial help waiting for you.

Glossary

The ACT: A standardized test produced by ACT, Inc. for college admissions in the United States.

The Advanced International Certificate of Education (AICE): An international curriculum that prepares students in the upper levels of high school for college and future employment.

Advanced Placement (AP): A program that places a high school student in a college-level course.

Bachelor's Degree: The academic degree that colleges or universities give students after studying for four years.

Board of Admissions: A committee that collectively determines whether or not an applicant is eligible to become a student at their university.

Community College: A junior college that offers courses to local students.

Community Service: Non-paying, voluntary work that is performed for the benefit of society.

Doctorate: The highest academic degree that colleges and universities give students.

Dual Enrollment: When a student is enrolled in two or more academic institutions — generally, a high school student taking college courses.

Extracurricular Activities: Activities outside the scope of regular curricula (such as journalism, sports, or volunteer work).

Fraternity: A society of male students at a college or university.

Grade Point Average (GPA): The number that represents a student's average grade.

Graduate School: The part of a college or university that offers advanced academic programs for students who have already earned a bachelor's degree.

Grant: An amount of money given by an organization.

Guidance Counselor: A person employed by an academic institution to help students plan for the future.

International Baccalaureate (IB): An international educational foundation that offers educational programs for children between the ages of 3 and 19.

Internship: A temporary position that offers on-the-job training instead of employment.

Ivy League Schools: A group of eight renowned private colleges and universities in the Northeastern United States. The institutions are Brown University, Columbia University, Cornell University, Dartmouth College, Harvard University, the University of Pennsylvania, Princeton University, and Yale University.

Master's Degree: The academic degree that colleges or universities give students after one or two years of additional study after earning their bachelor's degree.

The SAT: A standardized test used in the United States for college admissions.

Scholarship: An amount of money awarded by an organization to support a student's education.

Sorority: A society of female students at a college or university.

State College: A college that is financed by the state government.

Student Loan: Money leant at interest that is used to pay for a student's education.

Transcript: An official record that details the particulars of a student's work, including coursework and grades.

Undergraduate: A college or university student who has yet to earn a bachelor's degree.

Bibliography

Bauld, Harry, *On Writing the College Application Essay*, Collins Reference, Harper-Collins Publishers, New York, 2005.

Bodine, Paul, *Great Application Essays for Business School*, McGraw-Hill, New York, 2006.

Cohen, Katherine, *Rock Hard Apps: How To Write A Killer College Application*, Hyperion Books, New York, 2003.

Curry, Boykin et al. (eds.), *Essays that Worked for College Applications*, Ballantine, New York, 2003.

Ferguson, Margaret et al. (eds.), *The Norton Anthology of Poetry*, 4th ed., W.W. Norton and Co., New York, 1970. (193, 199)

Fifty Successful Harvard Application Essays, 2d ed., St. Martin's-Griffin, New York, 2005.

Hernández, Michelle A., *Acing the College Application: How to Maximize Your Chances for Admission to the College of Your Choice*, Ballantine, New York, 2002.

---, *A Is for Admission: The Insider's Guide to Getting into the Ivy League and Other Top Colleges*, Grand Central Publishing, New York, 2009.

Kramer, Stephen and M. London, *The New Rules of College Admissions*, Fireside Books, New York, 2006.

Mason, Michael. *How to Write a Winning College Application Essay, Revised 4th Edition*, ©2000 Michael James Mason, Prima Publishing, Rosevale, CA, 2000.

Rankin, Estelle and B. Murphy, *Writing an Outstanding College Application Essay*, McGraw-Hill, New York, 2005.

Spencer, Kathleen, *Writing as Thinking/Thinking as Writing*, Unpublished, © Kathleen L. Spencer, January 2008.

Untermeyer, Louis (ed.), *The Concise Treasury of Great Poems*, Simon and Schuster, New York, 1953. (411)

Van Buskirk, Peter, *Winning the College Admission Game*, Peterson's, Lawrenceville, NJ, 2007.

Author Biography

I am a proud grandmother (aka "Nonnie") of my beautiful granddaughter Aubrey, a just as proud mother of Jessica and Michael, and a wife. Career wise, I am the Career and College Center Specialist and Scholarship Coordinator for a local high school in our county. I actually added on the position of Scholarship Coordinator myself, because I found the results of winning scholarships so fascinating and rewarding for my students, and much of my scholarship work is done during my own time at home. Our students have won the most awards for the past 15 out of 16 years over the other six schools in our district since I began working with scholarships, averaging over $6 million yearly for the past five years, and I have given countless lectures and workshops, weekly private meetings with parents and students, and have been interviewed on several local and national radio stations. Some of my awards received for my work with scholarships include the County School Employee of the Year in 2000 and 2004, as well as District Teacher of the Year for the VFW several times (even though I am not a teacher), and multiple nominations for several Who's Who organizations for professionals and business leaders.

Besides my family, scholarships and helping students are my passions in life, and both are something I will continue to do, even after retirement.

Index